IMAGO DEI

D1599774

IMAGO DEI

Human Dignity in Ecumenical Perspective

EDITED BY THOMAS ALBERT HOWARD

THE CATHOLIC UNIVERSITY OF AMERICA PRESS
Washington, D.C.

Library of Congress Cataloging-in-Publication Data
Imago Dei : human dignity in ecumenical perspective / edited by
Thomas Albert Howard.
pages cm
Includes bibliographical references and index.
ISBN 978-0-8132-2143-4 (pbk. : alk. paper)
1. Theological anthropology—Christianity   2. Dignity—Religious
aspects—Christianity.   3. Image of God—History of doctrines.
I. Howard, Thomas A. (Thomas Albert), 1967–
BT701.3.I45 2013
233'.5—dc23
2013003479

CONTENTS

What is man that Thou art mindful of him?

Psalm 8:4

IMAGO DEI

INTRODUCTION

THOMAS ALBERT HOWARD

THE years following World War II witnessed much discussion about and reflection on the idea of human dignity. In 1949, with the Holocaust and the Nuremberg trials fresh in mind, the drafters of the new West German constitution, or *Grundgesetzt*, included in its opening article the statement that "the dignity of man is inviolable." A year earlier, the United Nations' Universal Declaration of Human Rights referred to the "inherent dignity" of human beings and proclaimed that "all human beings are born free and equal in dignity and rights." In the 1960s and 1970s, numerous constitutions drafted in the wake of decolonization also made reference to human dignity. In various speeches and writings, Martin Luther King appealed to the term as did Václav Havel and other signatories of Charter 77, a key document protesting the oppressive political climate of Czechoslovakia during the cold war. What is more, drafters of the constitution of the European Union affirmed that their union "is founded on the values of respect for human dignity." In short, the post-1945 moral-political landscape, in the West and in the world generally, has been powerfully shaped by appeals to human dignity.[1]

The origins of this moral vocabulary have various sources, but few would deny that it owes an immense historical debt to the biblical, Judeo-Christian notion of human beings as created in the image of God (Hebrew: *tselem Elohim;* Greek: *eikon Theos;* Latin: *imago Dei*). Indeed, for Christians today, irrespective of confession or denomination, the language of dignity has been employed to express the invaluable worth of the human person as bearing the impress of divinity. The ultimate biblical rationale is found in Genesis 1:26–27: "Then God said, 'Let us make man in our image, according to our likeness.... So God created man in his own image, in the image of God he created him; male and female he created them." Commenting on this passage in his *On the Creation of Man,* the Eastern Church Father Gregory of Nyssa exulted that "everything about him [man] manifests royal dignity, by his exact likeness to the beauty of the archetype."[2] For John Calvin, "God's image is the perfect excellence of human nature."[3]

From the early church to the sixteenth century to the present, appeals to the image of God and a concomitant assertion of hu-

1. Teresa Iglesias, "Bedrock Truths and the Dignity of the Individual," *Logos* 4 (2001): 114–34. One could also point to developments in recent decades. As David Brooks has written: "The quest for dignity has produced a remarkable democratic wave. More than 100 nations have seen democratic uprisings in the past few decades. More than 85 authoritarian governments have fallen. Somewhere around 62 countries have become democracies, loosely defined." See David Brooks, "The Quest for Dignity," *New York Times,* January 31, 2011.

2. Quoted in Andrew Louth, ed., *Ancient Christian Commentary on Scripture, Genesis:1–11,* vol. 1 (Downers Grove, Ill.: IVP Academic, 2001), 34.

3. John Calvin, *Institutes of the Christian Religion,* vol. 1, trans. Lewis Battles (Philadelphia: Westminister Press, 1960), 190.

man worth or dignity have been constants in Christian moral reflection about the human person, even if Christian practice has sadly fallen far short of Christian principle. But as those who have preoccupied themselves with human dignity in recent years can attest, the principle, even the word "dignity," is not always easy to get a handle on, and it faces a number of complex challenges today, at both a practical and a theoretical level.

Etymologically understood in its Western context, dignity (*dignitas*) arguably owes more to classical than to Christian thought: in the Roman world *dignitas* was the amount of personal clout that a male citizen acquired throughout his life—a concept we might today associate more with "esteem" or "prestige." It possesses a hierarchical, aristocratic connotation that does not sit easily in our democratic age.[4]

What is more, for sociobiologists, and for ethicists who take their cues from sociobiology, there has been a tendency to collapse any distinction between human persons and the rest of sentient nature. A small but growing chorus of thinkers has even made the case against "human exceptionalism," charging others with the misjudgment of "speciesism": overvaluing the *humanum* at the expense of moral obligations toward animals. We must "widen the moral circle," Richard Ryder has argued, and overturn "a sentimental tendency to put ... our own species on a pedestal."[5]

When moral claims about the human person are made, they are usually made on liberal, broadly Kantian grounds, appealing to rationality, equality, autonomy, freedom, and tolerance. From this perspective, notions of the image of God and human dignity

4. Adam Schulman, "Bioethics and the Question of Human Dignity," in *Human Dignity and Bioethics: Essays Commissioned by the President's Commission on Bioethics* (Washington, D.C., 2008), 6–7.

5. Richard Ryder, "All Beings that Feel Pain Deserve Human Rights," *The Guardian*, August 6, 2005. Cf. Joan Dunayer, *Speciesism* (Lantern Books, 2004).

appear somewhat nostalgic, religious residues oddly sedimented in our contemporary moral discourse. It is perhaps not surprising then that before his death the Nobel-winning writer Czeslaw Miłosz ruefully asked about the perdurability of the ideas behind "those beautiful and deeply moving words which pertain to the old repertory of the rights of man and the dignity of the person." He elaborated: "I wonder at this phenomenon because maybe underneath there is an abyss. After all, these ideas had their foundation in religion, and I am not over-optimistic as to the survival of religion in a scientific-technological civilization.... But how long will they stay afloat if the bottom is taken out?"[6]

The University of Notre Dame historian Brad Gregory has recently put the matter even more forcefully. "Rights and dignity can be real," he writes,

only if human beings are more than biological matter. The modern secular discourse on human rights depends on retaining in some fashion—but without acknowledging—the belief that every human being is created in the image and likeness of God, a notion that could be rooted in nature so long as nature was regarded as creation whether overtly recognized as such or not. But if nature is not creation, then there are no creatures, and human beings are just one more species that happened to randomly evolve, no more "endowed by their creator with certain unalienable rights" than is any other bit of energy-matter.[7]

While Gregory is keen to defend dignity, other contemporary thinkers seem prepared to dispense with the concept. Harvard University's Steven Pinker, in a critique of the President's Council on Bioethics' report, "Human Dignity and Bioethics" (2008), for instance, offers an assessment that would appear to confirm

6. Milosz as quoted by Mary Ann Glendon in "The Bearable Lightness of Dignity," *First Things* 213 (May 2011): 43.

7. Brad Gregory, *The Unintended Reformation: How a Religious Revolution Secularized Society* (Cambridge, Mass.: Harvard University Press, 2012), 381.

Miłosz's and Gregory's worst fears. Taking this report to task while criticizing the longstanding preoccupation with dignity by the council's initial director, Leon Kass,[8] Pinker argued that "dignity" is an inherently religious concept, "a squishy, subjective notion, hardly up to the heavyweight moral demands assigned to it."[9] Pinker's concerns echo those made earlier by the medical ethicist Ruth Macklin, who argued in a much-discussed article that "dignity is a useless concept in medical ethics and can be eliminated without any loss of content."[10] Those participating in the moral reasoning of Macklin and Pinker might not necessarily always eschew the word "dignity," but they are more likely to ground it, not in an innate God-given essence, a substantive theological anthropology, but in human beings' highly developed capacities for rationality and autonomy (Kant again). The latter terms are presumably more areligious and hence more palatable within a liberal, pluralistic democracy and among those beholden to philosophical naturalism with its purely immanent understanding of human identity.

In an age of biotechnology, the theologian Gilbert Meilaender identifies two specific threats to the idea of human dignity. A rightly constituted Christian anthropology, he argues, views the human person as "neither beast nor God," but somewhere in between, invested with the image of the Creator, but still a creature. If this is the case, then in our age we are prone to violate our dignity in two ways. We can see ourselves entirely as beasts, the sum of our ap-

8. See Leon Kass, *Life, Liberty, and the Defense of Dignity* (San Francisco: Encounter Books, 2002). Cf. Lawrence Vogel, "Natural Law Judaism? The Genesis of Bioethics in Hans Jonas, Leo Strauss, and Leon Kass," *The Hastings Center Report* 36 (May–June 2006): 32–43.

9. Steven Pinker, "The Stupidity of Dignity," *The New Republic*, May 28, 2008, 28–31.

10. Ruth Macklin, "Dignity Is a Useless Concept," *British Medical Journal* 327 (December 20–27, 2003): 1419–20.

petites played out in a field of genetic "predestination," albeit perhaps psychopharmacologically enhanced. But we can also err by attempting to remake ourselves into more-than-human, demigods, neo-Gnostics, who view the body as little more than a disposable shell for our "brains" or "mind." At the extreme end of this line of thinking, one finds advocates of "transhumanism" or "posthumanism," enthusiasts for an almost unlimited re-engineering of body and brain through the promises of biotechnology. While many stop short of the "brave new world" posited by posthumanists, Meilaender feels that as a culture we are already a long way down the road of seeing the body not as the "place" of personal identity, but merely as a "resource" for it—a foreboding development, he believes.[11] Francis Fukuyama argued along similar lines in his much-discussed book *Our Posthuman Future: Consequences of the Biotechnology Revolution* (2002).[12]

Much more could be said about the idea of human dignity and its present-day quandaries and detractors. But in light of the state of public discussion about this topic, let me state the animating, simple question for this book: *How might Christians today think well and wisely about human dignity?* Further, what do different traditions of Christian thought have to say about the idea of human dignity, especially in light of the shared biblical notion that human beings are made "in the image and likeness of God." Does this notion necessarily recommend the moral language of human dignity? And how have various recent historical forces and developments (the rise of biotechnology, yes, but also processes of glo-

11. Gilbert Meilaender, *Neither Beast nor God: The Dignity of the Human Person* (New York: Encounter Books, 2009).

12. Francis Fukuyama, *Our Posthuman Future: Consequences of the Biotechnology Revolution* (New York: Farrar, Straus & Giroux, 2002). Cf. Michael Sandel, *The Case Against Perfection: Ethics in the Age of Genetic Engineering* (Cambridge, Mass.: Harvard University Press, 2007).

balization, terrorism, intractable problems of poverty and disease, the proliferation of moral and economic choices made available to individuals in liberal societies) affected the manner in which we think and speak about human dignity?

In an effort to address these broad questions, this book (derived from a conference by the same name) brings together voices from three major families of Christianity: Eastern Orthodox, Catholic, and Protestant.[13] In other words, the chapters that follow bear witness to a deliberately ecumenical enterprise. All contributors have been asked to speak *from their own tradition:* what distinctive resources from their tradition might provide assistance to other Christians in thinking wisely and well today about human dignity? But each has also been asked to address how their tradition encourages (or might discourage?) an inviting and compelling *public* language about the scope and meaning of human dignity? When Christians speak of human dignity, in other words, must they necessarily "preach to the choir" or might their language of human worth be rendered in an idiom accessible to those who do not share their faith commitment? As some of the reflections that follow imply (particularly by the contributors' tendency to focus more on the sources of dignity in *imago Dei* teachings than on dignity per se), there might be limitations to this seemingly desirable enterprise, for the Christian revelation has profound implications for the very meaning and *telos* of the human being.

13. The conference took place on the campus of Gordon College (Wenham, Massachusetts) on April 16, 2010. In coming together for Christian-ecumenical purposes, we recognize the abiding importance of Christian-Jewish conversation on the same topic. After all, it is the Hebrew Scriptures from which Christians derive much of their own conception of human value. On specifically Jewish approaches to human dignity, see Doron Shulziner, "A Jewish Conception of Human Dignity," *The Journal of Religious Ethics* 34 (December 2006): 663–83, and Daniel S. Nevins, "Gadol Kvod Habriot: Placing Human Dignity at the Center of Conservative Judaism," *Judaism: A Quarterly Journal of Jewish Life and Thought* 54 (Summer–Fall 2005): 188–93.

Under the rubric of these broader questions, contributors were initially asked to entertain some more specific ones. While the degree to which these were taken up vary considerably among the authors, and some were understandably elided or ignored to tighten an essay's focus, the reader might benefit from considering them, at least to get a sense of the "touchstone" concerns animating the book. As is evident, many highlight the ecumenical nature of this endeavor. Herewith:

1. Does human dignity require theological or transcendental foundations or can it be understood in purely immanent terms?

2. Does the historic Protestant emphasis on Original Sin diminish human dignity? Does teaching on the Fall, in other words, mean that certain aspects of human dignity were forfeited and can only be attained again through "divine grace"?

3. How does the Catholic natural law tradition figure in discussions of human dignity, and how might other, non-Catholic Christians participate in (or perhaps raise questions about) ideas about natural law?

4. How does the Orthodox notion of *theosis* (the "divinization" of humankind through Christ's redemptive work) affect discussions of human dignity, and ought this teaching be embraced (or questioned) by non-Orthodox Christians?

5. How might *ecumenical* thinking about human dignity be translated into robust *interreligious* dialogue about the same concept?

6. Does the language of human dignity provide a rallying point for greater ecumenical collaboration among Christians, or does it bring to the surface abiding theological differences and divisions?

A summary should not substitute for the thing itself, but to give the reader some guideposts for the essays that follow, brief sketches of each author's contribution might prove helpful.

In the first chapter, "The Promise of the Image," Father John Behr, approaching the topic from an Eastern Orthodox standpoint, offers a profoundly Christological reading of the *imago Dei*. He makes his case in dialogue with ancient Greek Fathers, such as Gregory of Nyssa, and contemporary Orthodox theologians, such as David Bentley Hart. Although all human beings have a certain baseline dignity, which ought to be respected as such, Christ alone "is the image of the invisible God, the first born of all creation" (Col 1:15) and all Christians are enjoined to accept a path of *theosis,* literally becoming godlike—something Orthodox Christians regard as distinctive to their tradition.[14] (Behr assiduously avoids using the term *theosis,* although the idea is implied throughout his essay.) Even amid well-intentioned efforts to affirm contemporary notions of human dignity and human rights in liberal political discourse, Christians should remember, argues Behr, that "we have yet to become human, in the stature of Christ—who is the image of God—[and who] has revealed [this] to us within this world." Or as St. Irenaeus put it, "the work of God is the fashioning of the human being." Behr's contribution offers a bracing challenge to anyone who might want to understand the notion of *imago Dei* immanently or instrumentally, as a rationale for a political order or touchstone for a particular political or social discourse. Christ alone fully illumines the image of God, and the true, eschatological vocation of the human person—humankind's "manifest destiny," if one will—is compromised when it settles for anything less than the path of radical, purifying sanctification set before us in the New Testament and in the writings of the Church Fathers.

In chapter 2, "Toward an Adequate Anthropology: Social Aspects of *Imago Dei* in Catholic Theology," Russell Hittinger offers reflections from the perspective of a Thomist philosopher and legal

---

14. On *theosis* generally, see Russell Norman, *Fellow Workers with God: Orthodox Thinking on Theosis* (Crestwood, N.Y.: St. Vladimir's Seminary Press, 2009).

scholar with particular expertise in the development of post-1789 Catholic social thought and moral theology. Hittinger calls attention to a complex, promising development in modern Catholic social teaching: to what degree can corporate entities—such as a married couple, a family, a voluntary organization, or, not least, the church itself (that is, not individuals alone)—bear witness to the *imago Dei*? Do corporate entities exhibiting what John Paul II called "true society," in fact, exhibit the image of God at a fuller, more complete level than an individual person? Alluding to a question posed by Leo XIII (1878–1903), Hittinger asks: "What would be missing from the world if the [modern] state reduced all dignities to individuals and to a single, homogenous social form of citizenship?" He pursues this question—and several variations on it—as it has been taken up in subsequent papal encyclicals, in the documents of the Second Vatican Council, and, particularly, in the writings of John Paul II and Benedict XVI. Since "man is the image of an inscrutable divine communion of persons [i.e., the Trinity]" then it stands to reason, Hittinger concludes, that forms of human community and social solidarity exhibit the divine image at once differently and perhaps at a higher level than individuals alone. In the grand sweep of Catholic thought, Hittinger recognizes that this is a relatively recent development and one that stands in some tension with past theological reflection preoccupied more with the individual person as imaging the Godhead. Even so, Hittinger thinks it to be a highly important and promising development and one that other, non-Catholic Christians can and should both learn from and perhaps contribute to.

In the final chapter, C. Ben Mitchell offers us "The Audacity of *Imago Dei*: The Legacy and Uncertain Future of Human Dignity." A Baptist layman and a bioethicist by training, Mitchell, more directly than the other contributors, focuses attention on some of the contemporary challenges to human dignity encountered in the realm of biotechnology. "Advances in genetic engineering, pre-implantation genetic diagnosis, cybernetics, robotics, and nano-technology depend in large measure on our willingness as a culture to recast what it means to be human," he writes. He then catalogs a number of moral quandaries presented by the biotechnological revolution, including some that were taken up in recent years by the President's Council on Bioethics, established under the presidency of George W. Bush in 2001. While cautiously optimistic about the promise of many technologies, Mitchell makes clear that "brave new world" scenarios cannot be dismissed as mere fear-mongering. He then turns to Christian resources—particularly scriptural, Protestant, and specifically Baptist ones—that offer, as he puts it, a "creation anthropology" that provides a robust defense of "human exceptionalism" against those who want to chart or are resigned to accept a "posthuman" or "transhuman" future. While agreeing with Behr that "Christians find the dignity of the human person made most manifest in Jesus of Nazareth," they cannot dispense with the creational dignity of every person, even in the absence of special revelation. While Protestantism (especially in its Calvinist guises) is often known for accenting the doctrine of Original Sin, it possesses, too, a robust doctrine of creation. This should be remembered today and employed to "reinvigorate" the "meaning and use" of the idea of human dignity. Even so, Original Sin, as Protestant thinkers from Martin Luther to Reinhold Niebuhr have made clear, helps us recognize that "grotesque" detractions from human dignity can manifest themselves even when—perhaps especially when—the loftiest of intentions are hitched to some of the most promising advances in human knowledge.

Introductions, like guests, should not outstay their welcome. But allow me, in conclusion, to repeat one of the questions originally posed to the contributors: "Does the language of human dignity provide a rallying point for greater ecumenical collaboration among Christians, or does it bring to the surface abiding theological differences?"

Whatever one finally makes of the term "dignity," my earnest hope is that this slim volume will help facilitate "greater ecumenical collaboration," a deepening of fraternal unity and mutual understanding about a topic of first-order significance for all Christians, indeed all people. This should not mean, though, that the reader ought to expect a clear convergence of opinion or some grand synthesis of viewpoints. If anything, what we have here is a sincere effort at a conversation—and an open-ended one at that, as the chapters make clear and as Gilbert Meilaender underscores in his afterword.

What is more, unity, as the wisest ecumenists remind us, does not mean uniformity. It does mean, however, making every effort possible to learn from one another in a joint endeavor to search out the mind of Christ. Put differently, I hope this book exhibits what some have called "receptive ecumenism," which is rightly distinguished from "false irenicism" (see John Paul II, *Ut unum sint*), a least-common-denominator ecumenism that papers over genuine and abiding differences—perhaps even vitiating ecumenism in the name of promoting it.[15] Instead, "receptive ecumenism" attempts to *learn from the very particularity of the other;* insofar as possible, it tries to see developments in different traditions as a *potential gift.* It asks the question, formulated by Paul Murray, of not only what might I teach others, but "what can we learn, or receive, with integrity from our various [Christian] others in order to facilitate our own growth together into deepened communion in Christ and the Spirit."[16]

15. On this topic, see Thomas Oden, *The Rebirth of Orthodoxy: New Signs of Life in Christianity* (San Francisco: HarperSanFrancisco, 2003), 55–68.

16. Paul Murray, ed., *Receptive Ecumenism and the Call of Catholic Learning:*

Most readers interested in this book, I suspect, will share a desire for a "deepened communion in Christ and the Spirit" among Christians whose collective memories and divisions stretch back to 1054 and 1517. As the 500th anniversary of the Protestant Reformation draws near, these divisions continue to scandalize the church and diminish her witness in the world. The words of Karl Barth, a Protestant, as quoted approvingly by Hans Urs von Balthasar, a Catholic, ring true: "If we listen to Christ, we do not live above the differences that divide the churches but in them. [Which leaves us with one painful alternative:] We should not try to explain the multiplicity of churches at all. We should treat it the way we treat our own sin and those of others: *as sin*. We should treat it as part of our guilt.... [We] can only be *shocked* by these divisions and *pray* for their elimination."[17]

In the final analysis, then, this book is offered in the spirit of a prayer, an effort to bring divided Christians together, to search out together the mind of Christ, our shared first love and final end. Accordingly, allow me to offer a reflection from John Paul II in his encyclical *Ut unum sint* (1995):

I am reminded of the words of Saint Cyprian's commentary on *the Lord's Prayer*, the prayer of every Christian: "God does not accept the sacrifice of a sower of disunion, but commands that he depart from the altar so that he may first be reconciled with his brother. For God can be appeased only by prayers that make peace. To God, the better offering is peace, brotherly concord and a people made one in the unity of the Father, Son and Holy Spirit." At the dawn of the new millennium, how can we not implore from the Lord, with renewed enthusiasm and a deeper

---

Exploring a Way for Contemporary Ecumenism (Oxford: Oxford University Press, 2008), ix.

17. Barth as quoted by Hans Urs von Balthasar, *The Theology of Karl Barth: Exposition and Interpretation,* trans. Edward T. Oakes, S.J. (San Francisco: Ignatius Press, 1992), 4–5.

awareness, the grace to prepare ourselves, together, to offer this *sacrifice of unity?*

Or, as our Lord Himself prayed: "The glory that you have given me I have given to them, that they may be one even as we are one, I in them and you in me, that they may become perfectly one, so that the world may know that you sent me and loved them even as you loved me" (Jn 17:21–23, RSV).

I would like to express a special thanks to the Lilly Fellows Program at Valparaiso University; a grant from this fine organization helped underwrite this project. In particular, I would like to thank the program's board members and its staff, including Mark Schwehn, Joe Creech, and Kathy Sutherland. These folks command my abiding respect and admiration.

I would also like to express ongoing gratitude for the Lilly Endowment itself, and specifically its Program for the Theological Exploration of Vocation for helping support this and many other endeavors of the Critical Loyalty project at Gordon College.

Several Gordon College faculty members, staff, alumni, and students deserve a hearty word of thanks for their contributions to this project. Accordingly, I thank Greg Carmer, Ian Marcus Corbin, Stan Gaede, Joshua Hasler, Bruce Herman, Daniel Russ, Hilary Sherratt, Timothy Sherratt, John Skillen, and Bruce Webb. Above all, I thank Debbie Drost and M. Ryan Groff. Their many gifts and competencies enable projects such as this one actually to come to completion.

Finally, I thank, once again, my cherished, wordsmithy wife, Agnes R. Howard. She read the whole manuscript several times and provided invaluable advice and criticism.

[1]

THE PROMISE OF
THE IMAGE

JOHN BEHR

THAT human beings are important is something
we take for granted, and not only because we are
human beings (or so we think—more on this later).
It is a theme that has provoked reflection since time
immemorial, and not only for us human beings: the
question of the Psalmist—"What is man that thou art
mindful of him?" (Ps 8:4, 144:3; cf. Jb 7:17; Heb 2:6)—
presumes that no less than God himself recognizes
our worth! However, over recent decades, the subject
of human dignity has become very controversial, especially as it has come to be utilized as a mainstay in
arguments about bioethics. "Dignity," Harvard University's Steven Pinker argues, is a "squishy, subjective notion, hardly up to the heavyweight moral demands assigned to it." It is a vague concept employed

uncritically, he further claims, by those who wish to advance an "obstructionist bioethics" in a neutral moral language that in reality rests upon prior religious convictions. Moreover, he insists, not only does it not add anything to the discussion, but it is in fact potentially harmful, as the perception of "dignity" resides in the eye of the beholder: "Every sashed and be-medaled despot reviewing his troops from a lofty platform seeks to command respect through ostentatious displays of dignity."[1]

Now, what from a Christian perspective marks out the dignity of human beings is that, unlike the rest of creation (and even the angels), they alone are created in the image and likeness of God. This statement, of course, requires a lot of unpacking, both in respect of its content and also, and perhaps more importantly, in regard to the hermeneutic by which we can make the statement. Its content has been explicated in a variety of ways over the centuries. But it is striking that the typically twentieth-century manner of restating its content—that it is *as persons* that human beings are in the image of God—resorts to the very same point upon which Pinker and others would attempt to rest their moral arguments. As Pinker puts it, "Even when breaches of dignity lead to an identifiable harm, it's ultimately autonomy and respect for persons that give us the grounds for condemning it."[2]

"Autonomy and respect for persons." Such language may well seem to be far less indebted to or based upon a Christian heritage: we are all "persons" regardless of our race, creed, or status. It would seem to be an eminently humanistic claim. It is the first of the "self-evident" truths proclaimed by the Declaration of Independence (1776), that "all men are created equal, that they are

1. Steven Pinker, "The Stupidity of Dignity," *The New Republic*, May 28, 2008, 28–31.

2. Ibid.

endowed by their Creator with certain unalienable Rights, that among these are Life, Liberty and the pursuit of Happiness." And it is universally applied by the United Nations' Declaration of Human Rights (1948), again as the first item: "All human beings are born free and equal in dignity and rights. They are endowed with reason and conscience and should act towards one another in a spirit of brotherhood."

But are these truths in fact self-evident? They are not empirically verifiable, and in fact they fly in the face of our own daily observation. Yet despite the great inequality into which human beings are born—in disparate conditions, economic, social, physical, and intellectual—we would nevertheless surely still want to say that there is something about every human being *as a person* that is absolute, equal, and irreplaceable. But because this conviction is not an empirical conclusion, nor even empirically verifiable, it is an a priori assumption, or, in other words, a statement of faith.

HUMAN NATURE AND THE "CHRISTIAN REVOLUTION"

David Bentley Hart has recently argued a spirited case that this absolute value placed upon each human being *as a person* is not, as the fashionable enemies of Christianity are wont to assume, the result of an enlightened, civilized society breaking free from the bondage of religion in the name of reason, so that if the value ascribed to the person is an a priori, it is at least one of reason. Hart argues that, quite to the contrary, the very notion of the person is in fact a result of the revolution that is Christianity. He gives the example, for instance, of Peter in the Gospels, in whom, as Erich Auerbach noted, we can see "the image of a man in the highest and deepest and most tragic sense" compared to the portraiture of the great classical writers. Yet that he is nothing but a

Galilean peasant is not only not good taste but an act of rebellion, in which "we see something beginning to emerge from darkness into full visibility, arguably for the first time in our history: the human person as such, invested with an intrinsic and inviolable dignity, and possessed of infinite value."[3] The very fact that we habitually and unthinkingly speak of all human beings as "persons" is a testimony to the impact that the Christian revolution has had, for to "have a person," strictly speaking, was a right which Roman law bestowed only upon citizens—slaves were human beings lacking personhood (*non habens personam*). ⟋

For Christians in the ancient world, the Gospel was literally a message of liberation in a manner we can barely begin to comprehend today. Christ had triumphed over the powers of this world, all the things to which human beings had subjected themselves but which Christ had shown to be nothing: the elemental spirits of the universe; things which have no power over us, but to which we give subservience; things which are not but which hold us in thrall (such as, today, our "market forces")—his triumph has tamed the fearful world in which humans had formerly lived. That God created the world ex nihilo emphasized the absolute tran- ⟋ scendence of the Creator, who in reverse was now experienced as immanent within creation; and creation itself was understood as a gratuitous expression of divine love, a place of beauty and wonder, whose diversity reflected the multifaceted splendor of God's own wisdom, and thus a subject worthy of our inquisitiveness. And that the drama of salvation is enacted within this world, working backward to the beginning and forward to the eschaton, gives the time of creation a meaning and an orientation.

It is within this new world created by the Christian revolution,

3. David Bentley Hart, *Atheist Delusions: The Christian Revolution and its Fashionable Enemies* (New Haven, Conn.: Yale University Press, 2009), 167.

Hart argues, that our notion of "person" emerges, particularly in the context of the debates about the person and nature of the Incarnate Son of God. As Hart writes,

The rather extraordinary inference to be drawn from this doctrine [of Chalcedon] is that personality is somehow transcendent of nature. A person is not merely a fragment of some larger cosmic or spiritual category, a more perfect or more defective expression of some abstract set of attributes, in light of which his or her value, significance, legitimacy, or proper place is to be judged. This man or that woman is not merely a specimen of the general set of the human; rather, his or her human nature is only one manifestation and one part of what he or she is or might be. And personality is an irreducible mystery, somehow prior to and more spacious than everything that would limit or define it, capable of exceeding even its own nature in order to embrace another, ever more glorious nature. This immense dignity—this infinite capacity—inheres in every person, no matter what circumstances might for now seem to limit him or her to one destiny or another. No previous Western vision of the human being remotely resembles this one, and no other so fruitfully succeeded in embracing at once the entire range of finite human nature, in all the intricacy of its inner and outer dimensions, while simultaneously affirming the transcendent possibility and strange grandeur present within each person.[4]

The result of all the intense theological reflection in the controversies that beset the church from the fourth to the eighth centuries, over matters which Edward Gibbon famously dismissed as turning upon an iota, was a "coherent concept of the human as such, endowed with infinite dignity in all its individual 'moments,' full of powers and mysteries to be fathomed and esteemed ... an unimaginably exalted picture of the human person—made in the divine image and destined to partake of the divine nature—without

4. Ibid., 211.

thereby diminishing or denigrating the concrete reality of human nature, spiritual, intellectual, or carnal."[5] Something profound happened, resulting in a new, and radically different, way of looking at the world and understanding ourselves.

Hart is clear that this was not an immediate result, nor that every supposedly "Christian" society lived up to this reality. But, as he points out:

It required an extraordinary moment of awakening in a few privileged souls, and then centuries of the relentless and total immersion of culture in the Christian story, to make even the best of us conscious of (or at least able to believe in) the moral claim of all other persons upon us, the splendor and irreducible dignity of the divine humanity within them, that depth within each of them that potentially touches upon the eternal. In the light of Christianity's absolute law of charity, we came to see what we formerly could not: the autistic or Down syndrome or otherwise disabled child, for instance, for whom the world can remain a perpetual perplexity, which can too often cause pain but perhaps only vaguely and fleetingly charm or delight; the derelict or wretched or broken man or woman who has wasted his or her life away; the homeless, the utterly impoverished, the diseased, the mentally ill, the physically disabled; exiles, refugees, fugitives; even criminals and reprobates. To reject, turn away from, or kill any or all of them would be, in a very real sense, the most purely practical of impulses. To be able, however, to see in them not only something of worth but indeed something potentially godlike, to be cherished and adored, is the rarest and most ennoblingly unrealistic capacity ever bred within human souls. To look on the child whom our ancient ancestors would have seen as somehow unwholesome or as a worthless burden, and would have abandoned to fate, and to see in him or her instead a person worthy of all affection—resplendent with divine glory, ominous with an absolute demand upon our consciences, evoking our love and our reverence—is to be set free from mere elemental exis-

5. Ibid., 213.

tence, and from those natural limitations that pre-Christian persons took to be the very definition of reality.[6]

This is indeed a most remarkable and inspiring vision. What especially strikes one is the way Hart focuses on examples which are weak and broken, on the instances where we would rather turn our faces (rather like the disciples at the Passion), preferring instead our idea and ideals of what constitutes human dignity and divine existence.

But a vision which reverses the terms, as it were, by a divine exchange—to see divine strength in human weakness, eternal life in death, and the very Logos of God in flesh—is always going to appear a folly and a scandal to human thought. It will necessarily be a fragile vision, one that is all too easily forgotten. And so, Hart concludes with a troubling question:

How long can our gentler ethical prejudices—many of which seem to me to be melting away with fair rapidity—persist once the faith that gave them their rationale and meaning has withered away? Love endures all things perhaps, as the apostle says, and is eternal; but as a cultural reality, even love requires a reason for its preeminence among the virtues, and the mere habit of solicitude for others will not necessarily survive when that reason is no longer found. If, as I have argued ... the "human" as we now understand it is the positive invention of Christianity, might it not also be the case that a culture that has become truly post-Christian will also, ultimately, become posthuman?[7]

This may not necessarily be so, but there doesn't appear to be much cause for thinking otherwise. Having abandoned the notion of "dignity," even Pinker resorts to a "respect for persons," without giving any real reason for this.

Hart's typically sharp posing of the question does indeed give us pause for thought. But is it really the case that the "personal"

6. Ibid., 214.   7. Ibid., 215.

dimension of human existence, as we understand it today, is really the fruit of the Christian revolution? And is this indeed the best way to think of human dignity? Is being "human" to be equated with being a "person," as this has come to be understood today?

It is unquestionable that the primary category in terms of which we understand ourselves today is as "persons." And it is also clear that how we understand this—"endowed with infinite dignity in all its individual 'moments,' full of powers and mysteries to be fathomed and esteemed," as Hart puts it—differs from previous generations, betraying the fact that the term "person" has its own history and evolution: human self-understanding, the human experience of self, of being a person, has changed throughout the ages, as it changes throughout the life span of a single human being (a version of Ernst Haeckel's recapitulation theory, that "ontogeny recapitulates phylogeny"). As Charles Taylor notes, "There is some truth in the idea that people always are selves, that they distinguish inside from outside in all cultures." But he elaborates, "The really difficult thing is distinguishing the human universals from the historical constellations, and not eliding the second into the first so that *our particular way* seems somehow inescapable for humans as such, as we are always tempted to do."[8]

Unlike a statement of anatomy (that we have a head attached to a body, for instance), the articulation of our "personhood" is necessarily self-interpretative and self-referential, and necessarily specific, bound to a particular age—of the person concerned or the period of human history with which we are concerned—and

---

8. Charles Taylor, *Sources of the Self* (Cambridge, Mass.: Harvard University Press, 1989), 112.

to a particular cultural experience. And because of this, Taylor suggests, "no satisfactory general formula can be found to characterize the ubiquitous nature of a self-interpreting animal." Perhaps it is impossible by definition: the human being as a "self-interpreting animal" will be like Heraclitus's river.

It seems that our tendency to project our current understanding of ourselves as "persons" into a universal and atemporal reality has also been operative in some trends in contemporary theology. Some theologians, such as Jürgen Moltmann and Cornelius Plantinga, have argued that the term "hypostasis" as developed by the Greek Fathers provides a fundamental insight into the "personal" existence of God, and thus the grounding of all reality in the person. It is intimately connected with the divine "perichoresis": the three persons that the one God is, existing in perfect unity within one another, "a zestful wondrous community of divine light, love, joy, mutuality and verve," in which there is "no isolation, no insulation, no secretiveness, no fear of being transparent to another."⁹ This "social" model of the Trinity is then held up as the perfect model for human beings, created in the image of God, to strive to replicate on earth, overcoming our limited "individualism" to enter into community of truly personal communion. The adequacy of such claims with respect to the Greek Fathers has increasingly been called into question, as has also the methodology of this approach: it takes the concept of perichoresis, understood as that which make three to be one, fills it out with ideas borrowed from our own experience of relationships and relatedness, projects it onto God and then reflects it back onto the world as an excit-

9. Cornelius Plantinga, Jr., "Social Trinity and Tritheism," in R. J. Feenstra and C. Plantinga, Jr., eds., *Trinity, Incarnation and Atonement* (Notre Dame, Ind.: University of Notre Dame Press, 1989); quoted in Karen Kilby, "Perichoresis and Projection: Problems with Social Doctrines of the Trinity," *New Blackfriars* 81 (2000): 432–45, at 435.

ing previously underutilized resource of Christian theology that resolves our contemporary problem of "individualism" and gives new life to ancient, little-understood conceptual formulae.[10]

Other theologians, most notably Karl Rahner, have been much more circumspect regarding the term "person." He pointed out that while in antiquity the term "person" signified directly the distinct subsistence, and the rational nature of a particular being only indirectly, "the 'anthropocentric turn' of modern times requires that the spiritual-subjective element in the concept of person be understood."[11] Accordingly, he argued for using the phrase "mode of subsistence" rather than "person" to translate the Greek word *hypostasis:* we cannot change how people hear the word "person," and so need to use a periphrastic construction (but we can no more change a pattern of speech either!).

A further point that should be made is that the Greek Fathers of the fourth century were very reticent to speak of *three* persons or hypostasis. In fact, St. Basil says we should not use numbers at all:

When the Lord delivered [the formula of] the Father, Son and Holy Spirit, he did not make arithmetic a part of this gift! He did not say, "In the first, the second and the third" or "In one, two and three." But he gave us the knowledge of the faith that leads to salvation by means of holy names. So that the faith is what saves us; numbers have been devised as symbols indicative of quantity.... Count if you must, but do not damage the faith by doing so. Either by silence honor the ineffable things, or piously count the holy things. There is one God and Father, one Only-Begotten Son, and one Holy Spirit. We proclaim each of the *hypostases* singly (μοναχῶς); and if we must use numbers, we will not let an ignorant arithmetic lead us astray to the idea of polytheism.[12]

10. Kilby, "Perichoresis and Projection."

11. Karl Rahner, *The Trinity,* trans. J. Donceel (Tunbridge Wells: Burns & Oates, 1986), 108.

12. St. Basil the Great, *On the Holy Spirit,* 18.44–45. Ed. and French trans.,

We proclaim each singly, his point is, because they are incommensurable with each other; there is nothing in their individuating properties—being the unbegotten Father, the only-begotten Son, and the Spirit who proceeds—which would enable us to count three persons. As Vladimir Lossky points out:

> In speaking of three hypostases, we are already making an improper abstraction: if we wanted to generalize and make a *concept* of the "divine hypostasis," we would have to say that the only common definition possible would be the impossibility of any common definition of the three hypostases.[13]

In other words, it is not possible to specify what is common to each of the hypostases *as hypostasis*, as person—that is, what constitutes their personhood ("hypostasicity") in the abstract, before one applies the personal characteristics of Father, Son, and Spirit—because, being common to each, it would be classified as part of the *ousia*. And, Lossky further notes, although the Fathers did indeed articulate very clearly and precisely the relationship between hypostasis and *ousia*, the same cannot be said for a notion of the human person more generally: "For my part, I must admit that until now I have not found what one might call an elaborated doctrine of the human person in patristic theology, alongside its very precise teaching on divine persons or hypostases."[14]

If "dignity" is, as Pinker puts it, a "squishy, subjective notion," inadequate for serious moral reflection, then clearly the term "person," the term upon which even Pinker unthinkingly relies, is an even more flighty and evasive notion, a complex term with a history of continual evolution, changing throughout time and

B. Pruche, *Basile de Césarée: Sur le Saint Esprit,* rev. ed. SC 17 bis (Paris: Cerf, 2002). Eng. trans. in the series Nicene and Post-Nicene Fathers (NPNF) 8.

13. "The Theological Notion of the Human Person," in V. Lossky, *In the Image and Likeness of God* (Crestwood, N.Y.: St. Vladimir's Seminary Press, 2001), 113.

14. Ibid., 112.

throughout our own lives. To claim that our notion of "person"
has its roots in the transformation of thought—the understanding of God, ourselves, and all creation—achieved by the Greek
Fathers as they learned to articulate the doctrine of the Trinity
and the hypostatic union of natures in Christ, is, I would argue, to
mistake form for content, and in a very real sense miss the point
altogether. The theological debates of the fourth to seventh centuries were not about defining a clearer notion of "the person" in the
abstract, but about defining ever more clearly what is to be said
about a particular person, the "one Lord Jesus Christ," who is fully
divine and fully human, without confusion, change, separation,
or division: one Lord Jesus Christ known in two natures, with the
properties of each concurring in one hypostasis or *prosopon*. It
is this one, about whom we speak in this way, who is important,
not the terms themselves and how they form part of a trajectory
which culminates in how we now think of ourselves.

THE HUMAN: A CHRISTOLOGICAL
APPROACH

If the terms "dignity" and "person" provide neither steady
ground nor clear content for an attempt to answer the question
of the Psalmist—"What is man that thou art mindful of him?"—
perhaps we should return directly to the notion of being human.
This is a more fundamental category than that of "person," and
does not depend upon subscribing to particular notions of "person"; even slaves in antiquity were human even if Roman law did
not ascribe to them the dignity of having a persona. And likewise
we accept that being human does not depend upon the ability to
think about oneself in a particular way, or even to exercise our human "rights" or realize our "potential."

Returning to the idea of being human also brings us back to

the notion of the image of God, for the two are directly correlated by Scripture: after making all the other creatures by his word alone, God announces his project: "Let us make *anthropos* in our image and likeness" (Gn 1:27). How this correlation between being human and being in the image of God has been understood also has a history. Over the past century, from Karl Barth onward, there has been an increasing tendency to explicate our existence as the image of God in terms of humans being relational beings, persons in relation imaging the Trinity of divine persons that is God. However, the Apostle Paul and the early Church Fathers following him were much more specific, and again focused on Christ: it is he, the apostle says, who *is* the image of the invisible God (Col 1:15), in whom the fullness of divinity dwells bodily (Col 2:9), so that we cannot see God anywhere else, by some other means. As Christ *is* the image of God, Adam, being made "in" or "according to" the image and likeness (κατ᾽εἰκόνα ἡμετέραν καὶ καθ᾽ὁμοίωσιν) already points to Christ; Adam is, as Paul puts it, "a type of the one to come" (Rom 5:14).

Very strikingly, the first Christian theologians to reflect on this, such as Irenaeus of Lyons and Tertullian, located the "image" directly in the body. How can it be located anywhere else, Irenaeus asked, if Christ is to be the visible image of the invisible God?[15] The perfect human being, according to Irenaeus, is "the commingling and the union of the soul receiving the Spirit of the Father and joined to the flesh which was molded after the image of God."[16] As the image is located in the flesh, Irenaeus differentiates between the image and the likeness, that which is acquired when the human being lives, in the Spirit, directed toward God. As he puts it:

15. St. Irenaeus of Lyons, *Against the Heresies* (*AH*) 2.7, 19; 4.6.6; 5.6.1. Translation in Ante-Nicene Fathers 1.

16. *AH* 5.6.1.

For in times long past, it was said that *anthropos* was made in the image of God, but it was not shown [to be so]; for the Word was as yet invisible, after whose image *anthropos* was created; and because of this he easily lost the likeness. When, however, the God Word became flesh, he confirmed both of these: for he both showed forth the image truly, himself becoming that which was his image, and he reestablished the likeness in a sure manner, by co-assimilating *anthropos* to the invisible Father through the Word become visible.[17]

Tertullian also focuses our attention on the body, by combining the two accounts of the creation of the human being given in Genesis (1:26–27; 2:7):

Whatever [form] the clay expressed, in mind was Christ who was to become human (which the clay was) and the Word flesh (which the earth then was). For the Father had already said to his Son, "Let us make man unto our image and likeness; and God made man," that is the same as "fashioned" [cf. Gn 2:7], "unto the image of God made he him" [Gn 1:26–27]—it means of Christ. And the Word is also God, who "being in the form of God, thought it not robbery to be equal to God" [Phil 2:6]. Thus that clay, already putting on the image of Christ, who was to be in the flesh, was not only the work, but also the pledge of God.[18]

Our body is not only the handiwork of God, being fashioned into the image and likeness of God, that is, of Christ who is to come, but also the "pledge" of God that this indeed shall come to pass.

It was no doubt partly their battle with "Gnosticism" that prompted Irenaeus and Tertullian to give such high dignity to the body in a manner unparalleled with the later tradition. Under the influence of theologians in Alexandria, the later tradition was much more likely to locate the image of God in human beings within their intellectual or noetic faculty, as that which dif-

---

17. *AH* 5.6.2.

18. Tertullian, *On the Resurrection of the Flesh* 6, ed. and trans. E. Evans (London: SPCK, 1960) (translation modified).

ferentiates human beings from irrational animals, but also, more importantly as that which relates us, as reasoning (*logikoi*) animals, to the Divine Logos. We were made in the image of God, St. Athanasius says, by being granted a share in the power of God's own Word, so that having "shadows" of the Word and being made *logikos,* we might be able to partake of the Word and live the life of blessedness in paradise.[19] This is not to deprecate the body, but to emphasize that, even if we live *in* the body (and there is no suggestion at all that it should or could be otherwise) our true life, imaging God, does not however reside in living *for* the body. But human beings preferred that which was closer to themselves, their body, and so made the body an idol, an obstacle to their knowledge of God—not because of its materiality, but because it had become the focus of our attention. Nevertheless, this being the case, the Word took a body so that we might regain knowledge of him through the body, again, not through the materiality of the body but through the works he does in the body (we see him as a man, but then ask: what manner of man is it that does such works—healing the sick, forgiving sins, raising the dead, and paradigmatically conquering death by his own death); and in this way we become part of his body, witnesses to the resurrection.

Although it is played out in numerous ways, the predominant perspective of the Christian tradition in the first millennium, with two exceptions, was to relate the creation of the human being in the image of God to Christ as the image of God, and to place this in eschatological perspective—we are created looking forward to, in anticipation of, as a type of Christ. The first exception were the Antiochene theologians such as Diodore of Tarsus and Theodore of Mopsuestia. Having separated the Old Testament from the

19. See St. Athanasius the Great, *On the Incarnation,* 3. Translation in NPNF 4.

New, they tended to explain Genesis 1:27 solely within the scope of the Old Testament, as the dominion that human beings were to have over creation, and in this are echoed by modern Old Testament scholars.[20] The other exception is Augustine, who deploys a range of psychological imagery relating the interrelated faculties of the human being to the members of the Trinity.

However it is we define what constitutes the existence of human beings as created in the image of God, we are still confronted with the anomaly that this truth is not at all self-evident, any more than our modern claims regarding the equality of human beings. St. Gregory of Nyssa, in his treatise *On the Making of Man*, asks this question quite directly:

> How then is man, this mortal, passible, short-lived being, the image of that nature which is immortal, pure, and everlasting? The true answer to this question, indeed, perhaps only the very Truth knows.... [But] neither does the word of God lie when it says that man was made in the image of God, nor is the pitiable suffering of man's nature like the blessedness of the impassible Life.[21]

Gregory goes on to suggest, "by conjectures and inferences," that the discrepancy should be understood in terms of the distinction between the statement of intent in Genesis 1:27ab—"God created *anthropos* in the image of God, in the image of God created he him"—and the actual action of God in Genesis 1:27c—"male and female created he them," which Gregory links to the second creation narrative, in which God fashions his creatures from mud.

20. Old Testament scholars frequently make the same claim, while admitting that this is based upon our knowledge of ancient Near East cultures in general, in which the king alone was understood to be the image of God, rather than anything within the Old Testament which might legitimize this interpretation. Cf. P. Bird, "'Male and Female He Created Them': Gen 1.27b in the Context of the Priestly Account of Creation," *Harvard Theological Review* 74.2 (1981): 140.

21. St. Gregory of Nyssa, *On the Making of Man*, 16.4. Trans. in NPNF 5.

While God's stated intention is to make a human being in his image, what came to pass in this world is the creation of males and females, which Gregory takes as a provisional measure, enabling us to grow to our full estate, God's original intention. He suggests, in other words, much as St. Maximus will do later, that although we are now indeed males and females, we are not yet truly human.[22]

In these writers, then, the truth of the human being is not found in protology, looking back to a lost golden age of perfection, but in the future stature to which we are called, the stature of humanity that Christ alone has manifested in this world: "Your life is hidden with Christ in God: when Christ who is our life appears, then you will also appear with him in glory" (Col 3:3-4). This perspective is held right through to the end of the Byzantine era. Nicholas Cabasilas, writing in the fourteenth century, also asserts that it is not Adam but Christ who is the first true human being in history:

It was for the new human being (*anthropos*) that human nature was created at the beginning, and for him mind and desire were prepared.... It was not the old Adam who was the model for the new, but the new Adam

22. In the cosmic vision of St. Maximus the Confessor, Christ's work has removed all the divisions and separations which characterize our present experience of created reality, and which have resulted from the misuse of the power given to us for the purpose of uniting all in Christ. Amongst these is the distinction between males and females: "First he united us in himself by removing the difference between male and female, and instead of men and women, in whom above all this manner of division is beheld, he showed us as properly and truly to be simply human beings (*anthropos*), thoroughly transfigured in accordance with him, and bearing his intact and completely unadulterated image." (See *Ambiguum* 41, trans. in Andrew Louth, *Maximus the Confessor*, The Early Church Fathers [London: Routledge, 1996]). Following the Apostle Paul (cf. Gal 3:28), St. Maximus asserts that in Christ the distinction between male and female is removed. The removal of this distinction means that in Christ, and only in him, can we see both men and women as what they truly are: human beings.

for the old.... For those who have known him first, the old Adam is the archetype because of our fallen nature. But for him who sees all things before they exist, the first Adam is the imitation of the second. To sum it up: the Savior first and alone showed to us the true human being (*anthropos*), who is perfect on account of both character and life and in all other respects.[23]

Not only is Christ the first true human being, but he is the model in whose image Adam, "a type of the one to come" (Rom 5:14), was already created.

And if it is through the Passion (understood by the opening of the Scriptures and the breaking of the bread) that the disciples finally come to know who Christ is, then it is likewise in and through our own taking up the cross that we come to manifest the image of God and become fully human. When St. Irenaeus penned that beautiful, and much-quoted, line, that "the glory of God is the living human being," he did not mean, as we might today, being a person in the fullness of all our rights and inner potential, all that it is to be "alive."[24] Rather, for St. Irenaeus, the "living human being" is the martyr, going to death in confession of Christ:

In this way, therefore, the martyrs bear witness and despise death: not after the weakness of the flesh, but by the readiness of the Spirit. For when the weakness of the flesh is absorbed, it manifests the Spirit as powerful; and again, when the Spirit absorbs the weakness, it inherits the flesh for itself, and from both of these is made a living human being: living, indeed, because of the participation of the Spirit; and human, because of the substance of the flesh.[25]

23. Nicholas Cabasilas, *The Life in Christ*, 6.91–94. Ed. and French trans. M.-H. Congourdeau, SC 361 (Paris: Cerf, 1990); Eng. trans. C. J. deCatanzaro (Crestwood, N.Y.: St. Vladimir's Seminary Press, 1974), where it is numbered as 6.12.

24. *AH* 4.20.7.

25. *AH* 5.9.2.

The strength of God is made perfect in weakness, and so, paradoxi-
cally, it is in their death, their ultimate vulnerability, that the martyrs bear greatest witness to the strength of God. Not that they reck-
on death to be a thing of no importance, but that in their confession
they are vivified by the Spirit, living the life of the Spirit, who absorbs the weakness of their flesh into his own strength. When the
Spirit so possesses the flesh, the flesh itself adopts the quality of the
Spirit and is rendered like the Word of God.[26] The paradigm of the
living human being is Jesus Christ himself, and those who follow in
his footsteps, the martyrs, broken flesh vivified by the Spirit.

We have a very graphic example of this in the "Letter from the
Churches of Vienne and Lyons to their Brethren in Asia and Phry-
gia," almost certainly written by Irenaeus himself.[27] During a great
and bloody persecution of Christians around Lyons in the late
170s, some Christians were taken to the arena, but they "appeared
to be unprepared and untrained, as yet weak and unable to endure
such a great conflict." About ten of these, the letter says, proved to
be "stillborn" or "miscarried," causing great sorrow to the others
and weakening the resolve of those yet to undergo their torture.[28]
However, these stillborn Christians were encouraged through the
zeal of the others, especially the slave girl Blandina, the heroine
of the story (more lines are devoted to her than to any other figure, and she is named, while her mistress remains nameless). She
personifies the theology of martyrdom based on Christ's words to
Paul: "My strength is made perfect in weakness" (2 Cor 12:9). Blandina is specifically described as so "weak in body" that the others
were fearful lest she not be able to make the good confession; yet

26. *AH* 5.9.3.
27. The Letter is preserved in Eusebius, *Ecclesiastical History* (*EH*) 5.1–2. Ed. and
trans. K. Lake, Loeb Classical Library (Cambridge, Mass.: Harvard University Press,
1980 [1926]).
28. *EH* 5.1.11.

[she] was filled with such power that even those who were taking turns to torture her in every way from dawn until dusk were weary and beaten. They themselves admitted that they were beaten ... astonished at her endurance, as her entire body was mangled and broken.[29]

Not only is she, in her weakness, filled with divine power by her confession, but she becomes fully identified with the one whose body was broken on Golgotha: when hung on a stake in the arena,

she seemed to hang there in the form of a cross, and by her fervent prayer she aroused intense enthusiasm in those who were undergoing their ordeal, for in their torment with their physical eyes they saw in the person of their sister him who was crucified for them, that he might convince all who believe in him that all who suffer for Christ's sake will have eternal fellowship in the living God.[30]

Through her suffering, Blandina becomes identified with Christ (she no longer lives, but Christ lives in her); her passage out of this world is both her birth and Christ's reentry into it. After describing her suffering, and that of another Christian called Attalus, the letter continues:

Through their continued life the dead were made alive, and the witnesses (martyrs) showed favor to those who had failed to witness. And there was great joy for the Virgin Mother in receiving back alive those who she had miscarried as dead. For through them the majority of those who had denied were again brought to birth and again conceived and again brought to life and learned to confess; and now living and strengthened, they went to the judgment seat.[31]

The Christians who turned away from making their confession are simply dead—their lack of preparation has meant that they are stillborn children of the Virgin Mother, the church; but strength-

29. *EH* 5.1.18.   30. *EH* 5.1.41.
31. *EH* 5.1.45–46.

ened by the witness of others, they also are able to go to their death, and so the Virgin Mother receives them back alive—finally giving birth to living children of God. The death of the martyrs, the letter says later on, is their "new birth," and the death of the martyrs is celebrated as their true birthday.[32]

St. Ignatius of Antioch also uses the language of birth with regard to his forthcoming martyrdom, and, even more strikingly, claims that only in this way will he become a human being. Writing to the Christians at Rome, he implores them not to interfere with his coming martyrdom:

It is better for me to die in Christ Jesus than to be king over the ends of the earth. I seek him who died for our sake. I desire him who rose for us. The pains of birth are upon me. Suffer me, my brethren; hinder me not from living, do not wish me to die. Do not give to the world one who desires to belong to God, nor deceive him with material things. Suffer me to receive the pure light; when I shall have arrived there, I shall become a human being (*anthropos*). Suffer me to follow the example of the passion of my God.[33]

Undergoing death in witness to Christ, the "perfect human being" or the "new human being," is a birth into a new life, for St. Ignatius, to emerge as Christ himself, a fully human being.[34]

We have yet to become human, in the stature that Christ—who is the image of God—has revealed to us within this world. Perhaps now we can hear with a renewed depth the final words of Christ from the cross in the Gospel of John: "It is finished" (Jn 19:30). He is not simply declaring that his earthly life has come to an end, but that rather the work of God is now "fulfilled" or

32. *EH* 5.1.63.

33. St. Ignatius of Antioch, *Romans*, 6. Ed. and trans. B. Ehrman, *The Apostolic Fathers*, 2 vols., Loeb Classical Library (Cambridge, Mass.: Harvard University Press, 2003).

34. St. Ignatius of Antioch, *Smyrnaeans*, 4.2; *Ephesians*, 20.1.

"completed." The divine economy, the whole plan of creation *and* salvation, told from this perspective, culminates at this point. The work of God spoken of in Genesis, creating "the human being [*anthropos*] in our image and likeness" (Gn 1:26–27), is completed here: as Pilate said a few verses earlier, "Behold, the man [*anthropos*]" (Jn 19:5). The work of God is complete, and the Lord of creation now rests from his work in the tomb on the blessed Sabbath. By himself undergoing the Passion as a man, Jesus Christ, as Son of God and himself God, fashions us *into* the image and likeness of God, the image of God that he himself *is* (Col 1:15). As St. Irenaeus put it, "The work of God is the fashioning of the human being [*anthropos*]."[35]

CONCLUSION

The first point I would make is that all these claims are again not part of an empirically verifiable discourse. They are statements of faith and therefore interpretative statements. That Blandina appeared in the likeness of Christ was, one can be sure, not something noticed by the Roman pagans sitting around the amphitheater: all they saw was another case of a tragically deluded figure being torn apart by the beasts. It is only those in the arena, struggling alongside her in the faith, who were able to see Christ in her. And more to the point, they saw this as an encouragement for each of them to endure all the trials that befell them, to be born to true life in the Virgin Mother. Or, to be more precise, it is Irenaeus, the author of the letter, who sees things this way, who interprets the events he witnessed in the light of Christ, who sees in Blandina a figure of Christ, and describes her as such for our benefit.

The second point I would make is that, in the light of the ob-

35. *AH* 5.15.2.

servation just made, we acknowledge the point made by St. Gregory of Nyssa, that looking around us we do not directly see "images of God" everywhere, but men and women living broken lives, suffering, falling sick, and ultimately dying. However, rather than say that despite these empirical conditions, each of them is a person and so to be respected as such, it would be better to allow our interpretation of what we see to be conditioned by the light of Christ, so that we can say that what we see are images of God being fashioned, human beings in the making. All the toils and turmoils of the sea of life provide the framework and the means by which we grow into the stature of human nature manifest in Christ himself, the broken, suffering servant. As the epistle of Barnabas puts it so pithily: "Human beings are earth that suffers" (ἄνθρωπος γὰρ γῆ ἐστιν πάσχουσα).[36] It is therefore primarily in those who would previously not have been recognized—the autistic child, the mentally ill, the physically challenged, the derelict, homeless, imprisoned—that we see what it is to be human, and in so doing, and responding to them, that we become human ourselves. This is the dignity of being human, a dignity which will never stand upon itself, but will always sacrifice itself.

But, again, this is a statement of faith. And it is one that Hart rightly suggests has changed the world, inspiring a new creation. As we have yet to become human, it is not the case that a post-Christian world will be posthuman, but it may well lose its aspirations to become human.

36. Barnabas, *Ep.* 6.8. In Ehrman, *The Apostolic Fathers.*

TOWARD
AN ADEQUATE
ANTHROPOLOGY

SOCIAL ASPECTS OF *IMAGO DEI*
IN CATHOLIC THEOLOGY

F. RUSSELL HITTINGER

IN his encyclical on ecumenism, *Ut unum sint,* Pope
John Paul II made clear a desire that the Catholic magisterium might serve to enrich and deepen the
faith of all Christians. The reflections that follow on
Catholic social doctrine—a key focus of the magisterium in the modern age—are offered in this same
spirit, inviting Christians of various confessional and
denominational loyalties to think *with*—if understandably not always in full agreement—the Catholic
Church, in the hope that "visible unity" among divided Christians might, in the fullness of time, become
an actual reality.

It is of considerable importance, however, to realize that Catholic social doctrine was not developed in the intramural quarrels of the Reformation and Counter-Reformation. Rather it emerged in response to the new anthropological and political creed of "man and citizen" that swept from France in 1789 to the rest of Europe and her former colonies in the late eighteenth and nineteenth centuries. This creed of "liberty, equality, and fraternity" considered the human person in two ways: first, as a being of nature, having natural liberties and rights which had been obscured or broken by the historical social order; second, as a citizen, standing equally among other citizens before the state. On this model, fraternity was associated preeminently if not exclusively with citizenship, for as Rousseau among others had argued, membership in the state reconstitutes the broken relations of nature and history. Other social memberships claiming their origins in nature, history, or divine revelation were deemed legitimate only insofar as they were either the private choice of individuals, or insofar as they were permitted or "conceded" by the state.

Catholic thinkers, both clerical and lay, quickly targeted the ideal of fraternity as the most troubling part of the new creed. Cardinal Chiaramonti of Imola (the future Pius VII, later kidnapped and held in solitary confinement by Napoleon), put on his letterhead: "Liberty, Equality, and Peace in our Lord Jesus Christ."[1] Throughout the nineteenth century, Catholic thinkers at-

1. On Chiaramonte, see E. E. Y. Hales, *Revolution and Papacy: 1769–1846* (Notre Dame, Ind.: University of Notre Dame Press, 1966), 107. For his part, Leo XIII contended that "liberty, equality and fraternity" had its grounding in the relations of the divine Trinity. *Humanum genus* (1884), §34; and *In plurimus* (1888), §14. By this polemical flourish, Leo did not mean to conflate nature and grace, much less to suggest that Christian Trinitarian theology is merely another way to restate the rights of man and citizen. Rather, he meant to remind his flock that they already have a more adequate understanding of these things.

tempted to identify social domains having a sacred solidarity not reducible to state citizenship. During the pontificate of Leo XIII (1878–1903), the pattern for Catholic social doctrine was well established. The church took a scissors-like approach to the state, limiting and contextualizing citizenship according to higher and lower social orders. From below, by marriage and family, and from above the church.

It was an ingenious strategy. In effect, the secular state, which publicly claimed to be desacralized, was pinioned by two facets of a sacramental system. By sacramental we mean not only sacraments in the ordinary sense of the term, like holy orders and marriage, which are instituted by Christ as sacraments of redemption; we also mean by sacrament whatever makes visible the invisible mysteries of God. In both the restricted and the broader sense of the term, sacraments are irreducibly social. There can be no such thing as a private or invisible sacrament. Regarding these social spheres, the church could say to the state, *noli me tangere*, "don't touch me." In its deepest pattern, Catholic social doctrine was a defense of the individual *in* society, but chiefly a defense of societies against the state's ambition to exercise a monopoly on fraternity. Arguments drawn from the economy of creation, such as natural law, and arguments drawn from the economy of redemption were thus marshaled, usually in tandem, to buttress this explicitly anti-Rousseauean conception of social orders representing divine things.[2]

2. For a compact account of this history, see *The Teachings of Modern Roman Catholicism: On Law, Politics, and Human Nature*, ed. John Witte and Frank Alexander, with introduction and chapter on Leo XIII by Russell Hittinger (New York: Columbia University Press, 2007). There, I put into context the Leonine response to issues of democracy, religion, and public order, especially the question of whether human authority can ever be free-standing without the primary authority of the eternal law. On the latter question, see also my essay "Pascendi Dominici Gregis

Genesis 1:26 teaches that the individual member of the species is a sacrament—speaking now in the broad sense of the term. In ⟍ the visible order of the hexaemeron, it is the individual man, male and female, who is made unto the image and likeness of God, and thus the individual member of the species is a locus of sacrality in the visible world. This idea, so familiar to Jewish and Christian theology, is much contested, even detested, in the secular world of late modernity. Our culture separates the value of the individual as self-determining from the individual's membership in a certain natural species or kind. A "person" is a pure thisness (as late medieval philosophers suggested, *haecceity*) in his liberty, and is counted as a "member" only by his own choice or consent.[3] The suspicion that membership without consent is a kind of servitude has in our era come to encompass more than what we would count as sociological reality. Choice replaces nature, and gender replaces sex. The late twentieth century champions what has been called a "negative anthropology."[4] We can say what man *is not,* for to affirm what he is limits freedom. Such a view radically upsets our traditional notions of philanthropy, which depend in some way upon our love of what we, as individuals, have in common by way of species. For example, in the Adamic wedding canticle of Genesis 2:23, Eve is recognized not only as an individual but as a fellow human, "bone of my bones, and flesh of my flesh."

100 ans après. Deux modernisms, deux thomismes: réflexions sur le centenaire de la Lettre contre les modernistes de Pie X," *Nova et Vetera* (January–March 2009), 45–69.

3. As the French philosopher Pierre Manent puts it, human nature for us is a cipher, an "efficacious indetermination" allowing a zone of liberty in which the individual can "affirm himself without knowing himself." Pierre Manent, *The City of Man*, trans. Marc A. LePain, with foreword by Jean Bethke Elshtain (Princeton, N.J.: Princeton University Press, 1998), 129.

4. The term "negative anthropology" is taken from Rocco Buttiglione, *Karol Wojtyla* (Grand Rapids, Mich.: Eerdmans, 1997), 53.

The Lutheran theologian Gilbert Meilaender rightly observes that Christianity teaches that the human person is "neither beast nor God." Man cannot be resolved into beast or pure spirit. But this does not imply that the person is a pure individual, deranged from any ranking according to species or kind. In late modernity, therefore, Christians can expect this central anthropological truth about the image of God to be rejected. Interestingly, this rejection is based not only on a denial of what the teaching presupposes in the order of divine revelation and the response of faith; it is also, if not primarily, based on a denial or a doubt about the natural locus of the creature without which a theology of revelation is bereft of its material sign.

Given the contemporary confusion about what belongs respectively to nature or grace, and given radical doubt about the individual's (moral) membership (as person) in a natural species, the question animating this chapter might seem doubly puzzling. Can social entities be said to exist in the image of God? In a theologically serious ecumenical readership such as the present one, I assume for the purpose of this inquiry the basic Christian teaching that the individual *human* person is made unto the image and likeness of God. Although there are a few qualifications to be made along the way, I set aside the need for any polemic or dialectic that gets us back, from scratch so to speak, to the starting point of Genesis 1:26. But with the traditional point of departure fully in view, my theme raises a question of considerable importance. What about social entities? As Paul teaches in Ephesians 5, the great sacrament, or mystery, is the analogical sign of the union of man and woman and of Christ and the church. While this reality cannot be constituted in the absence of real individual persons, the sign pertains to the union. To use again the example afforded by Genesis 2, Eve is affirmed as a fellow human individual, but, even so, the "union of one flesh" is not reducible to either Eve or Adam.

Doesn't this suggest that a defense of the dignity of the individual human person is a necessary but not a sufficient condition for an "adequate anthropology"?[5] Without its proper complement of social relations and ends, the *humanum* is vulnerable to ideologies and pseudosciences which adopt the principle of methodological individualism: namely, that social unities and relations among members can be reduced to nonsocial properties of members or composites thereof. Following this logic, the matrimonial union is reducible to aggregated individuals, and the individuals are reducible to isolated bits of desire and consciousness stripped of common species. In effect, the property and status of *being a member* would be counted as a mere fiction rather than a great sacrament. Needless to say, this method will not work for Catholic theology, which takes a realistic view of social entities, and what is more, regards social union as the crowning moment in both the orders of creation and redemption—to wit, marriage and church.

\ The Catholic understanding of "made unto the image and likeness of God" includes two distinct but related ideas—man as an individual member of a common species, and man as a member of a social communion—each in its own way manifesting something of the invisible God. A correct anthropology, then, has not one but rather two tasks. First, to articulate the good of being an individual human being. Second, to articulate how this good is perfected in being a member of a society or societies. Questions

5. I use the term "adequate anthropology" in the sense given to it by Pope John Paul II, who meant an integral anthropology—one commensurate to the whole human good. The pope used the term in many settings, but a first bevy of meanings is accessible in *Man and Woman He Created Them: A Theology of the Body,* translation, introduction, and index by Michael Waldstein (Boston: Pauline Books, 2006), in the index at 678.

of justice and love will inevitably track this twofold aspect of the human good.

My aim in this chapter is not to expound Catholic doctrine in the formal sense of the term. While I limit myself chiefly to sources which have some degree of magisterial authority within the church—pontifical letters, papal catechesis, conciliar documents, clarifications issued by curial offices—I do so in order to show the evolution and disposition of the questions and to call attention to an emerging pattern of answers. The resources bestride more than one sector of theology: biblical theology, Christology, sacramental theology, ecclesiology, moral theology (under which Catholic social doctrine is placed), and theological anthropology. This rich panoply of resources of itself constitutes a fabric of theology that is recognizably Catholic.

FRAMING TERMS AND QUESTIONS

At the beginning we need to briefly define some terms. Within the Catholic tradition, *imago* (a copy), *similitudo* (a likeness or perfection of an image), *imitatio* (a representation), *assimulatio* (a similarity in form), *conformatio* (a constitutional character), and *vestigium* (a trace) are theological terms of art.[6] Since Leo XIII, magisterial documents rely chiefly upon Thomas Aquinas's understanding of sacral imaging. I make no apology for using Thomas both in the text and the notes for the purpose of clarifying terms and distinctions. Since the Second Vatican Council, however, the neo-scholastic tradition has had a much looser hold over this subject. While they do not necessarily indicate where the discussion must end, the scholastic terms are often the best place to begin.

6. Frequently used in conjunction with the pronoun *quaedam* (a certain one), the adverb *quodammodo* (in a certain way or measure), the adjective *conveniens* (harmoniously or fittingly), and the verb *praefere* (to display).

It is commonly taught that *imago* pertains in an unqualified sense to Christ, who is *the* (eternal and consubstantial) image of the Father.[7] In the case of the created human person, who is an imperfect likeness, the proper description is drawn from Scripture: *ad imaginem et similitudinem Dei,* unto the image and likeness of God. The preposition indicates that the imprinted image in the human person is not one in being with its source. Thus, *imago* is in man only by an "analogy of proportion." What is the proportion? The proportion signified by *imago* is not just any created effect, but a "likeness in species," or a "likeness in nature."[8] Nothing, of course, participates directly by way of species or nature in divinity except the divine persons. In the human person, the participated likeness consists in acts of knowing and loving which are at the root of human nature—thus counting as likeness in species or nature. This pattern of knowledge and love manifesting from afar in the creature a likeness of divinity has been called the "image of representation."[9] Minimally, it refers to the human aptitude for God as a first principle of being and goodness. These are intimated in the creature's spiritual operations, principally self-possession and self-transcendence. From here below, we can see something excellent about the human being that deserves dignity.

It is also commonly taught that although human reason untutored by faith can detect within itself and in other human persons something divine-like in the operations of knowledge and love, the notion that the created person is an analogue of a trinity of divine persons can be grasped only by faith, and by sight only in glory. As Augustine said—and as Thomas reaffirmed—we *see* a

7. *Summa theologiae* (S.t.) I 93.1 ad 1.

8. S.t. I 93.2 c, and ad 4.

9. Here, I rely upon the discussion of image in Romanus Cessario, *Christian Faith & Theological Life* (Washington, D.C.: The Catholic University of America Press, 1996), 38–48.

trinity within ourselves, but we *believe* a trinity in the godhead.[10]
By adoption in baptism, and through actions informed by faith,
hope, and charity, we can grasp something of the community of
divine persons in the created image. Image of God, in the strict
Trinitarian sense, is in the public domain only by virtue of divine
revelation and the response of faith. This point always needs to
be underscored, for we often confuse a bottom-drawer notion of
human dignity (as something divine-like) with the strict idea of
being made unto the image and likeness of the Trinitarian God. It
needs reemphasis for another reason. As St. Irenaeus wrote:

In prior ages it was certainly said that man was made to the image of
God, but it had not appeared, since the Word was still invisible, to whose
image man had been made, moreover, for this reason the resemblance
was easily lost. But when the Word of God became flesh, he confirmed
the one and the other; he showed the image in all its truth, becoming
himself that which was his image, and restored the resemblance in a sta-
ble manner, rendering man completely like the invisible Father by means
of the Word, from then on visible.[11]

Finally, it is commonly taught that the term *similitudo* or likeness
can mean two things. A likeness can be something more general
than an image. All creatures have a certain likeness to God (*similitudo vestigii*) as vestiges or foot prints—that is to say, effects which
manifest a first cause. *Similitudo* can also mean the perfection of
an image. The likeness of the image is more perfect by acquisition

10. Furthermore, image in human persons is subject to different states or conditions. Man is made unto the image of God (1) by creation, which all have in common, (2) by grace of the New Covenant, and (3) in the likeness of glory. S.t. I 93.9.

11. St. Irenaeus of Lyons, *Against Heresies,* V, 16,2 (Sources Chrétiennes, 153,
216–17). I refer the reader to the International Theological Commission document *A
la Recherche D'Une Ethique Universelle: Nouveau Regard Sur La Loi Naturelle* (2008).
It explains very nicely how the theme of the image of God is located, in part, but
not in its entirety, under natural law. See especially 5.1, "The Incarnate Logos: Living
Law," and note 91 on St. Irenaeus.

or infusion of certain habits. The perfection, whether by nature or grace, is not merely in the capacities to know and love, but in *operationes*—actions.[12] In fact, much depends upon how this distinction is rendered and applied. In this essay, we are usually dealing with the second sense of "likeness," which is to say the (moral) perfection of an image.

Within the scheme of Catholic theology, image falls directly under theological anthropology and Christology, while likeness (as a perfection of the image) falls under moral and sacramental theology, both of which pertain to actions perfecting the image— chiefly, actions in conformity to grace, but not excluding perfections derived from action in accord with the natural law.[13] At least in the Roman model, social doctrine attends to *similitudo*, the actions which perfect an image.

Now, having compressed into a few paragraphs several books of theology, we can begin to address the question whether image and likeness are predicated of a society. At the outset we can remove one option. If we mean that the image and likeness consist directly and properly in an accumulation of social relations, the answer is no. Augustine and Thomas reject, for example, the idea that Adam is not image until Eve, and that neither are images until the child.[14] Made unto the image of God, the human person is,

12. Ibid., ad 1. "Nor is it unfitting to use the term 'image' from one point of view and from another the term 'likeness.'" Ad 3.

13. "The service which moral theologians are called to provide at the present time is of the utmost importance, not only for the Church's life and mission, but also for human society and culture. Moral theologians have the task, in close and vital connection with biblical and dogmatic theology, to highlight through their scientific reflection that dynamic aspect which will elicit the response that man must give to the divine call which comes in the process of his growth in love, within a community of salvation. In this way, moral theology will acquire an inner spiritual dimension in response to the need to develop fully the 'imago Dei' present in man." *Veritatis splendor*, §111.

14. "As Augustine says (De Trin. xii, 5), some have thought that the image of God

according to St. John Damascene, an "intelligent being, endowed with free-will and self-movement." This dignity is sacral, because the soul is directly created by and ordered to God. The primary relation, therefore, is the created image entirely to its entire Trinitarian exemplar. As John Paul II has written on Adam's solitude in Genesis: "*Man is 'alone': this is to say that through his own humanity, through what he is, he is at the same time set into a unique, exclusive, and unrepeatable relationship with God himself*."[15] Society does not confer this primordial dignity. Rather, the face of God, as the Psalmist says, the "light of thy countenance," is signed upon the individual human person. No talk about a social *imago* can disturb this anthropological center nor extinguish its light.

Another hurdle, perhaps more apparent than real, to speaking of a social *imago* is the fact that a human social order does not enjoy a unity of substance. Augustine famously argued that some sign of the Trinity is found in the distinct but unified mental acts of memory, understanding, and love. The key to this argument is that the acts are one in nature, and this cannot be said of two or more human persons in a social union. If we are to speak of a social image, we need a real principle of unity; for where there is no unity, there is nothing to bear an image (not even dimly and from afar) of the exemplary, divine unity. Therefore, we can rule out right away using the term "image" of two or more things which are unified only by way of aggregation or composition. A heap of sand, a mob in the piazza, a queue at the subway stop share a certain propinquity of place and time, but the unity is entirely acci-

was not in man individually, but severally. They held that 'the man represents the Person of the Father; those born of man denote the person of the Son; and that the woman is a third person in likeness to the Holy Ghost, since she so proceeded from man as not to be his son or daughter.' All of this is manifestly absurd." S.t. I 93.6 ad 2.

15. "Solitude and Subjectivity," general audience of October 24, 1979. In *Man and Woman He Created Them*, 151.

dental. It is neither a substantial nor a social unity, and therefore cannot qualify as a natural, created analogue of the divine persons. But this prompts us to ask the question of whether social unions are mere aggregations.

FROM THE TIME OF POPE LEO XIII— NATURAL LAW AND IMITATION OF GOD

To be sure, a social union is nonsubstantial. Members of a society are not stripped of their individual, substantial unity by virtue of their union with others. The issue stands or falls on whether two or more human persons can enjoy a *communio personarum* that stands between a unity of substance and a mere unity of aggregation. Are social unions real without being substantial? The answer is yes, and it provides a toehold into a solution of how we can speak of social entities imaging God.

Leo XIII and his successors fashioned a solution to this problem in two steps. First, they appropriated Aristotle's understanding of a social unity of order, and grafted it onto Pseudo-Dionysius's formula, the good is self-diffusive (*bonum sui diffusivum est*). This step provided a general, natural law framework for understanding the sacral iconicity of social orders, at least insofar as the individual image acquires the perfection of similitude by being rightly ordered in a social body.[16] Second, Leo and his successors turned to sacramental theology in order to show how *some* social orders directly and properly are called *image.*

16. The standard CSD principles of solidarity, subsidiarity, and common good are situated within this general scheme. On social unities which are more than mere aggregation, see my work for the Pontifical Academy of Social Science: "The Coherence of the Four Basic Principles of Catholic Social Doctrine: An Interpretation," keynote address to the Pontifical Academy of Social Sciences, XVIII Plenary Session. Margaret S. Archer and Pierpaolo Donati, eds., *Pursuing the Common Good,* Pontifical Academy of Social Sciences, *Acta* 14 (Vatican City, 2008), 75–123.

We begin with the first context, that of philosophical anthropology and natural theology. A unity of order stands between unity of substance (a man, bird, or plant) and a unity of mere aggregation (a heap of sand, or a queue waiting for the tram). In a social unity of order (a marriage, family, college, or church) each individual retains his own identity and operations; yet the social whole is more than the sum of its parts. It counts as a subject, person, and agent in its own right. Lawyers and philosophers call this kind of entity a "moral person" or a "legal person," or even a "mystical body." John Paul II calls them interpersonal subjectivities. These and other such terms designate the unity of members in a nonsubstantial "body." A social entity has not only a common end, but also an intrinsic common good. Thomas calls it *communicatio in forma*—a shared form that marks its distinctive kind of union.[17] In this case, the "form" is nothing other than an "order" of common action.

Form of order distinguishes a society from other kinds of human intersubjectivity. A crowd at the shopping mall, or an audience at the opera, exhibits intersubjectivity without pursuing a common end through united action. A fully social intersubjectivity can also be distinguished from that of partners. Partners pool their resources for the purpose of increasing profit. But such pooling does not necessarily require common action, and its proximate end is a private yield cashed out to each partner rather than enjoyment of an indivisible common good. To be sure, any temporal society will institute common pools which render more secure certain resources. Nevertheless, even when a common pool is instituted and maintained by a society, the pool is aggregated and made fit for private use in a way that a social union cannot be.

17. S.t. I, 4.3.

The terms of this distinction in canon law are *universitas rerum,* which is an organization of things, and *universitas personarum,* a union of persons. This distinction is clear when we think of a parish, which in one sense is a unity of buildings, lawns, sprinkler systems, and so forth. At least in Catholic theology, a parish is also, and most properly, a union of persons.

When the Catholic social magisterium speaks of a "true society," it means two or more persons communicating in a common good that cannot be distributed or cashed out. The common good never exists as a private good, and therefore when someone exits a marriage or a polity or a church he cannot take away his private share. Courts understand perfectly well that they can divide and distribute the external properties, but not the marriage itself. It is not distributable in a quantitative sense of the term; and whatever is not distributable according to quantity possesses some real unity. In the case of divorce, therefore, the matrimonial society is not redistributed so much as dissolved or annulled.[18]

Take the example of a queue in front of a credit union: the individuals are *parts* of the queue, *partners* in the credit union, and *members* of St. Rita's parish. To be sure, human persons related as parts and partners exhibit sociability, but it is only in their relation as *members* that it is possible to speak of "society." A social union, as John Paul II insisted, is something more than a relation *alter apud alteram,* a side-by-side intersubjectivity. It will enjoy a common good—a form of reciprocal action—that is intrinsically valuable to each of its members. It's not pooled and then consumed so

18. "Just as the civic life denotes not the *individual* act of this or that one, but the things that concern the common action of the citizens, so the conjugal life is nothing else than a particular kind of companionship pertaining to that common action. Wherefore as regards this same life the partnership of *married persons* is always indivisible, although it is divisible as regards the act belonging to each party." In IV Scriptum super libros Sententiarum D. 37, qu. 1, a. 1, qu^a 3 ad 3.

much as it is participated in. Again, this unity is what distinguishes a common good from divisible common utilities.

Following Thomas Aquinas, Leo XIII and his successors took this Aristotelian rubric of a social unity of order and grafted it onto Pseudo-Dionysius. Dionysius held that creatures imitate God in a twofold manner: first insofar as each creature has its own perfection in the order of substance; second insofar as creatures cause good in others. Thus, the famous dictum: *bonum sui diffusivum est,* the good is diffusive of itself. The greater the good, the more it is communicable and shareable.

Leo and Pius XI were quite keen on this formula, and both of them used it frequently to explain the sacred dignity of social orders. Here, one example will suffice. In the first year of his pontificate, Leo issued a letter on the problem of socialism. On the issue of whether diversity and inequality have a social purpose, Leo writes:

For, He who created and governs all things has, in His wise providence, appointed that the things which are lowest should attain their ends by those which are intermediate, and these again by the highest. Thus, as even in the kingdom of heaven He hath willed that the choirs of angels be distinct and some subject to others, and also in the Church has instituted various orders and a diversity of offices, so that all are not apostles or doctors or pastors, so also has He appointed that there should be various orders in civil society, differing in dignity, rights, and power, whereby the State, like the Church, should be one body, consisting of many members, some nobler than others, but all necessary to each other and solicitous for the common good.[19]

Leo here is paraphrasing Thomas: "God wished to produce His works in likeness to Himself, as far as possible, in order that they might be perfect, and that He might be known through them.

---

19. *Quod apostolici muneris* (1878), §6.

Hence, that He might be portrayed [*repraesentaretur*] in His works, not only according to what He is in Himself, but also according as He acts on others, He laid this *natural law* on all things, that last things should be reduced and perfected by middle things, and middle things by the first, as Dionysius says."[20] Notice that Thomas uses the term "natural law" explicitly in connection with the twofold representation of God in creatures. Clearly, this is not the modern epistemological doctrine of natural law but the more ancient metaphysical one based upon *imitation*.

What exists simply in God is communicated to creatures in a multiform manner. Thus, a double *imitation or portrayal*. First, a diversity of created things, each having a good according to its participated being. Second, a diversity of created things imitating God insofar as they cause goodness in others—insofar as they bring into existence, through secondary causality, additional modes of participation among themselves and others. The superabundance of what exists in God *simply* is, in creation, most perfectly expressed in a varied manifold. Charity perfects a social principle embedded in the creation of angels and men: namely, one loves the good not only as it is possessed and owned, but even more as it is poured forth and communicated to many.[21]

According to the exhortation of Ephesians 5:1, "be ye imitators of God," the intellective creature loves the good precisely as it is communicated to many—as it is made common. And without a unity of order, we would have isolated, individual things (each having the good of its own being), but, all together, portraying nothing more than a quantitative accumulation. Against socialism and liberalism, Leo insisted that the natural law requires

20. He directly cites 1 Cor 12:28–29, but is paraphrasing Thomas, at S.t., Supplement, q. 34.1.

21. De caritate (De car) 2.

both the preservation of the individual good *and* the pouring forth [*diffundatur*] of the good in social relations.[22] As Charles de Koninck pointed out, "One cannot love the common good without loving its shareability with others. The fallen angels did not refuse the perfection of that good that was offered them, they refused its community."[23] For his part, Thomas Aquinas argued that one cannot become a citizen in either a temporal or a celestial society without a special virtue pertaining to the good precisely as shareable. Thus the two master virtues, general justice and charity, which pertain to the common good. Thomas held that as charity "may be called a general virtue in so far as it directs the acts of all the virtues to the Divine good, so too is legal justice, in so far as it directs the acts of all the virtues to the common good. Accordingly, just as charity which regards the Divine good as its proper object, is a special virtue in respect of its essence, so too legal justice is a special virtue in respect of its essence, in so far as it regards the common good as its proper object."[24]

The double imitation can also be considered in the light of the Trinity. In the Trinity, a community of persons communicate in a common form. According to revelation, this is a sui generis case of relations which are not accidental but substantial. In the creature,

22. At best, the Dionysian double imitation shows that the plurality of created substances and their reciprocal operations exhibit something of the godhead in two ways: by unity of substance and in new social unities by diffusion of the good. This formula is drawn from natural theology, and therefore does not establish or demonstrate either that God is a trinity of persons or that the intellective creature is an analogue. As a matter of historical fact, the Dionysian-Thomist position on the double imitation was deployed by Catholic thinkers who, of course, had ready to hand the Trinitarian theology in a proper sense of the term.

23. Charles de Koninck, "The Primacy of the Common Good against the Personalists," in *The Writings of Charles De Koninck*, trans. Ralph McInerny, vol. 2 (Notre Dame, Ind.: University of Notre Dame Press, 2009), at 79.

24. II-II, 58.6, and De car. 2. For a discussion of these texts in CSD, see my keynote address to the Pontifical Academy of Social Science.

however, communication in a substantial form would obliterate the individuals and remove their ability to cause good in others. Therefore, creaturely imitation of God exhibits two forms which cannot be confused or absolutely separated. Each form represents something of Trinitarian unity. The creature possesses (imperfectly and from afar) a likeness of image in the order of substantial form (the unity of the soul's operations), as well as an additional perfection or similitude insofar as he or she communicates with others in a social form.[25] Thus, two different, but correlative, ideas of unity and good. As Thomas said: "The creature is like God in unity, inasmuch as each creature is one in itself, and all together are one by unity of order."[26]

What would be missing from the world if the state reduced all dignities to individuals and to a single, homogenous social form of citizenship? Leo contended, it would be like angels without choirs—isolated entities which, individually in the order of substance, bear the divine image, but lack a diversity in communicating as a social form whereby gifts are given and received. Society, said Leo in *Rerum novarum* (1891), cannot be reduced to "one dead level."[27] It was audacious in 1878 not only to pull Dionysius's

25. "Then, too, a thing approaches to God's likeness the more perfectly as it resembles Him in more things. Now, goodness is in God, and the outpouring of goodness into other things. Hence, the creature approaches more perfectly to God's likeness if it is not only good, but can also act for the good of other things, than if it were good only in itself; that which both shines and casts light is more like the sun than that which only shines. But no creature could act for the benefit of another creature unless Plurality and inequality existed in created things. For the agent is distinct from the patient and superior to it. In order that there might be in created things a perfect representation of God, the existence of diverse grades among them was therefore necessary." Summa contra gentiles (Scg) II 45.4.

26. De potentia 3.16 ad 2. The individual person is good by virtue of "kind," but even better according to actions which communicate good to others. This is an ancient trope on the hexaemeron in which the Creator declares the whole to be "very good."

27. *Rerum novarum*, §17, Acta 11, 108.

treatise on angelic hierarchy out of the hat to respond to socialism; even more generally, Leo and his successors were advancing
an argument for normative social pluralism based upon a social
imitation of God.

Recall that in Genesis the individual acts of creation are
deemed "good" one by one. Yet the hexaemeral acts are crowned
by the relation of Adam and Eve. This order is deemed "very good." /
Something new is brought into existence. Not another substance,
but a unity of order whereby persons, through action, cause good
in one another. This diffusion of the good, in human persons, from
the beginning is marked by a matrimonial social union which is a
type of the church.

While Leo and Pius XI sometimes use the term *imago* of this
new relation, more often they use the term *similitudo*. Recall that
similitudo can mean the perfection of an image. The human person is made unto the image and likeness of God, first as regards
his very being, and second *sub specie societatis*.[28] In short, social
unions are the perfection of the image—they pertain to likeness,
presupposing image.[29] But, one might ask, if the social union is

28. *Quadragesimo anno* (1931), §84. The argument continues through §87, where
Pius picks up the thread of Leo's teaching on the diversity of associations. Because
order, as St. Thomas well explains, is unity arising from the harmonious arrange-
ment of many objects, a true, genuine social order demands that the various members of a society be united together by some strong bond. This unifying force is present not only in the producing of goods or the rendering of services—in which the
employers and employees of an identical industry or profession collaborate jointly—
but also in that common good, to achieve which all industries and professions together ought, each to the best of its ability, to cooperate amicably. And this unity will
be the stronger and more effective, the more faithfully individuals and the industries
and professions themselves strive to do their work and excel in it.

Pius's citation takes the reader to two places where Thomas develops the Pseudo-
Dionysian theme of a twofold likeness of creatures to God. In the first, taken from
Summa contra gentiles, Thomas lays out the principle of the *duplex imitatio,* in the
order of being and in the order of the good. Scg III.70–71.

29. *Divini redemptoris* (1937), §29. "It is society which affords the opportunities

not substantial doesn't this imply that it is accidental? The answer is yes, but perhaps not quite as one might suppose. We read and hear much today about a theology of communion that is "relational." For instance, in *Caritas in veritate,* Benedict XVI proposes that Catholic social doctrine "requires a *deeper critical evaluation of the category of relation.* This is a task that cannot be undertaken by the social sciences alone, insofar as the contribution of disciplines such as metaphysics and theology is needed if man's transcendent dignity is to be properly understood.... The Christian revelation of the unity of the human race presupposes a *metaphysical interpretation of the 'humanum' in which relationality is an essential element.*"[30] The recent statement by the Catholic church's International Theological Commission on man as the image of God asserts that the human person is "an essentially relational being."[31]

We will have more to say about these recent statements later in this chapter. Here, a brief clarification will have to suffice. In the scholastic tradition inherited by the modern popes, the terms "substance," "relation," and "habit" are drawn from Thomas Aquinas, who took and reworked Aristotle's categories. Within this scheme, accidents are not unimportant. For instance, all of the

---

for the development of all the individual and social gifts bestowed on human nature. These natural gifts have a value surpassing the immediate interests of the moment, for in society they reflect the divine perfection, which would not be true were man to live alone [*divinamque praeferunt in civili ordinatione perfectionem, quod quidem in singulis hominibus contingere ullo modo nequit*]. But on final analysis, even in this latter function, society is made for man, that he may recognize this reflection of God's perfection [*ut hanc divinae perfectionis imaginem*], and refer it in praise and adoration to the Creator. Only man, the human person, and not society in any form is endowed with reason and a morally free will."

30. *Caritas,* §§ 53, 55.

31. The International Theological Commission's document *Communion and Stewardship: Human Persons Created in the Image of God* (text approved *in forma specifica* and submitted to Joseph Cardinal Ratzinger, President of the Commission). Signed on July 23, 2004. Written in English. §10.

acquired and infused virtues are accidental under the rubric of "habit." One's unity with his or her spouse is accidental under the rubric of "relation." In all beings other than God, perfection depends upon the individual substance having the right accidents.

From the point of view of its substantial goodness a thing is said to be good in a certain sense, but from that of its accidental goodness it is said to be good without qualification.... A thing is called a being inasmuch as it is considered absolutely, but good, as has already been made clear, in relation to other things. Now it is by its essential principles that a thing is fully constituted in itself so that it subsists; but it is not so perfectly constituted as to stand as it should in relation to everything outside itself except by means of accidents added to the essence, because the operations by which one thing is in some sense joined to another proceed from the essence through powers distinct from it. Consequently nothing achieves goodness absolutely unless it is complete in both its essential and its accidental principles. Any perfection which a creature has from its essential and accidental principles combined, God has in its entirety by his one simple act of being.[32]

A social unity of order is not a substance, but rather an order in which the right relations and habits exist as accidents, which is to say, as perfections, in the individual members. Precisely because social unities are not substances, the same individual can be a member of more than one social body without moving from substance to substance. But he or she certainly needs the appropriate habits and relations to participate as a member in this or that society. This is the key to understanding why social relations and their proper habits come under the notion of *similitudo*—likeness as a moral perfection of what is made unto the image of God.

To return to the main thread of our discussion, Catholic social doctrine contended that by suppressing and homogenizing social

---

32. *De Veritate*, q. 21, a. 5

relationships other than citizenship, the modern state was at war with a sacred order of things. Insofar as the state permitted the existence of other social entities only by the concession and in the pattern of state sovereignty, the state was implicitly claiming to be the exemplary cause of the good. Social entities are, in effect, icons or copies of the state. We should not underestimate how widely and deeply Catholic thinkers since 1789 depicted the modern state as a neo-pagan expression of state sovereignty.

As for liberalism, the social magisterium typically complained that the second prong of the Dionysian formula is either denied or obscured—diffusion of the good, for liberalism, is only an aggregate result ensuing upon self-interested action, such as the "hidden hand" of the market. Beneficence arises even in the absence of benevolence. We might think of Hayek's notion of "catallaxy," a spontaneous order in which a general good is attained without anyone intending to do so. This model preserves, perhaps, the dignity of the individual in the abstract, but does not affirm the perfection of the image in social unity. So, if the total state is a demonic rival to the divinity, the liberal state is a demonic rival to the diffusion of the good via social unions which represent, however inchoately, the divine Trinity.

The scissors-like approach positions issues of polity and public order within social sacralities of nature and grace. Except for a few notable exceptions (mostly in the 1960s), magisterial documents will include these three components: 1) a problem touching upon the state, 2) a discussion of what stands higher than the state, and 3) a discussion of what is lower. Take *Dignitatis humanae* (1965), the very tersely worded declaration on religious liberty. The council begins with the question whether the state may legitimately either command or prohibit acts of religion; it then makes a natural law argument for the inviolability of conscience not only as the individual stands before God but also in communal worship, family, and education; and it ends with the liberty of the church instituted by Christ, which of course goes beyond natural law warrants for liberty from the state. The freedom of the church "is the fundamental principle in what concerns the relationships between the Church and governments and the whole civil order."[33]

The scissor-like approach is important both for what it affirms and what it denies. It denies that any social-political order is legitimate if it proceeds from, or leads inevitably to, social homogeneity. As we have seen, undifferentiated equality can be achieved in two ways: the first by a kind of atomism, where individual persons are recognized but their social memberships are regarded as mere aggregations; the second by a kind of socialism, where individual persons possess no moral standing until and unless they are made members of a politically constructed community. In either way, "democracy" is not sustainable as a legitimate social "form." Pius XII made this clear in his Christmas address of 1944, *Benignitas et humanitas* (True and False Democracy). "If, then, we consider the extent and nature of the sacrifices demanded of all the citizens, especially in our day when the activity of the state is so vast and decisive, the democratic form of government appears to many as a postulate of nature imposed by reason itself." But, he warned, "the state does not contain in itself and does not mechanically bring together in a given territory a shapeless mass of individuals. It is, and should in practice be, the organic and organizing unity of a real people. The people, and a shapeless multitude (or, as it is

---

33. Preeminently, the church's freedom is not the *cura religionis* or the *cura iuris* but the care for the salvation of men, *quantum salus hominum curanda requirat* (DH, §13). See my paper presented to the 2011 meeting of the Pontifical Academy of Social Science: "Political Pluralism and Religious Liberty: The Teaching of *Dignitatis Humanae.*"

called, 'the masses') are two distinct concepts."[34] Without adherence to both prongs of the Dionysian understanding of natural law—the good of created persons, and the good diffused in social relationships by free action—there can be no authentic social form at all. Moreover, social forms which privatize what *Dignitatis* calls the "fundamental principle," the social form of the church, are at odds with both nature and grace.

IMAGE AND SACRAMENT

Now we must move along from the general pattern of imitating God *sub specie societatis,* to a more specific one—*in specie sacramenti,* with respect to a sacramental image. Leo's *Arcanum divinae* (1880) and Pius's *Casti connubii* (1930) were the two most important teachings on matrimony since the Council of Trent. Leo and Pius contended with state laws on civil marriage and divorce which were driven by the proposition that, by nature, marriage is only a collaboration for the purpose of reproduction. Matrimony, on that view, has no fixed, or what Leo called "insculpted," form. Therefore, the form of union falls entirely under the state's law, either by way of a direct imposition or by way of what the law allows individuals to decide.[35] It is not difficult to

34. *Benignitas et humanitas* (True and False Democracy), AAS/37 (1945), at 13–14.

35. *Casti* §49, 558. Pius writes: "To begin at the very source of these evils, their basic principle lies in this, that matrimony is repeatedly declared to be not instituted by the Author of nature nor raised by Christ the Lord to the dignity of a true sacrament, but invented by man. Some confidently assert that they have found no evidence of the existence of matrimony in nature or in her laws, but regard it merely as the means of producing life and of gratifying in one way or another a vehement impulse; on the other hand, others recognize that certain beginnings or, as it were, seeds of true wedlock are found in the nature of man since, unless men were bound together by some form of permanent tie, the dignity of husband and wife or the natural end of propagating and rearing the offspring would not receive satisfactory provision. At the same time they maintain that in all beyond this germinal idea mat-

appreciate why the social form of matrimony was of great interest to Catholics. For without an *insculpted form* marriage cannot be a natural sign of union of Christ and his church. In short, marriage would not be sacramental in the sense required for the sacramental economy of the New Covenant.

Citing Thomas, Pius XI contends that marriage is not merely a consent to the joining of bodies with a reproductive end in view. Rather, marriage is a consent to a certain union upon which ensue the ends.[36] Marriage is not a free-floating set of ends or purposes, but ends brought about through a specific mode of union. As Thomas taught: "Nor is the direct object of consent a husband but union with a husband on the part of the wife, even as it is union with a wife on the part of the husband."[37] Psychologically, one desires and chooses *this* man or woman. It could also be true that one has in view a mutually agreeable end, such as reproduction, economic security for the wider family, etc. But it is the consent *to the union* that enables the societal form and deserves to be called marriage. The other intentions—to consent to *this* man or woman, and to consent to a common end—can obtain in the absence of matrimony. Indeed, partnerships of various kinds, including partnerships that create a common pool of resources, will often entail a consensus (this person rather than that person) for such

---

rimony, through various concurrent causes, is invented solely by the mind of man, established solely by his will."

36. *Arcanum* and *Casti* are interrelated in more than one way. In the first place, Pius XI issued *Casti* as a reprise of Leo XIII's *Arcanum,* which he wished to "affirm" and to "expound more fully" (*Casti* §4, 540). Thematically, their nucleus is identical. As Pius said, Leo meant to vindicate the "divine institution of matrimony" and to defend the "perpetual stability of the marriage bond, its unity and firmness" (§5, 540). Citing Thomas, Pius insisted that marriage is consent to the union (*essentialibus proprietatibus subiciatur*), and should there be anything compatible with the union it is not true matrimony (*non esset verum matrimonium*) for the ends are already contained in the form. (§5, 541–42, citing S.t. III, Suppl. 49.3.)

37. In IV Sent. D. xxvii, qu. 1, a. 2, qu^a 1 ad 3.

and such an end without implying consent to a societal union.[38]

Reworking these very texts, Pius XI writes that while the begetting and education of children are first in the order of ends, they are not first in the form that makes matrimony: "This mutual molding [*interior conformatio*] of husband and wife, this determined effort to perfect each other, can in a very real sense, as the Roman Catechism teaches, be said to be the chief reason and purpose of matrimony, provided matrimony be looked at not in the restricted sense as instituted for the proper conception and education of the child, but more widely as the blending of life as a whole and the mutual interchange and sharing thereof."[39] He argues that marriage depends upon a "generous surrender of his own person made to another for the whole span of life."[40] Because its social form is instituted by God, Pius asserts that marriage is "more sacred" than the state.[41]

Yet, it is more sacred for another reason. Matrimony is the natural fundament of the sacrament, the sign of the unity of Christ

38. Thus, Thomas insists, with his typical brevity that reaches to the heart of the question, that matrimony is not merely the joining of minds or bodies, but rather that "the joining together of bodies and minds is a result of matrimony." In IV Sent. D. XXVII q. 1, a. 1. The essentials: one man and one woman, consenting to a perpetual union, consummated by a one-flesh act of unity.

39. Ibid., §24, 548f.

40. Ibid., §9, 543. Marriage is a "union of souls" that makes it entirely different from the "union of animals." In the old *Codex Iuris Canonici* (1917), still in place during Pius's pontificate, canon 1081 §2 defined matrimonial consent as the mutual exchange of "perpetual and exclusive rights to the body [*ius in corpus*], for those actions that are of themselves suitable for the generation of children." In isolation, the canon is perplexing because it does not include the purpose of education; what is more, the phrase *ius in corpus* could suggest the propinquity-of-organs position against which Leo and Pius had been arguing. In fact, the revised *Code* (1983) would rework this canon to reflect Pius's definition of marriage as self-gift: "an act of will by which a man and a woman by an irrevocable covenant mutually give and accept one another for the purpose of establishing a marriage." (CIC [1983] can. 1057 §2.)

41. *Casti* §69, 565.

and the church.[42] In the case of marriage, the material sign is already a social union (it is the only one of the seven sacraments that has a social unity of order as its natural sign). By grace, this social union is called *imago Christi*. Pius calls it a "living image" and an "efficacious" and "mystical image" of the whole Christ, Head and members.[43] Importantly, Pius insists that husband and wife bear the image by reciprocation. It has to be done together.[44] At least under the sacrament, neither the husband nor the wife alone are the image, but the union itself. For the sacrament, methodological individualism cannot suffice—namely, that social unities and relations among members can be reduced to nonsocial properties of members or composites thereof. So, here we have at least one instance of a social entity that is not just a perfection of the individual image, but one that is itself the bearer of an image.

We should not be surprised that Catholic social doctrine has regularly and insistently turned to the issue of matrimony. It is not, in the first place, a question of moral theology. Rather, it is the original case of a social union, precisely as a society, bearing

42. From the beginning, God "sealed" and "insculpted" in this union the two *proprietates* of unity and indissolubility. (*Arcanum* §5, 12f.) This reference to a law insculpted is taken from Thomas's idea of *lex indita*, which is to say, a law that moves its subject by communicating an inherent form. In the case of marriage, what is indicted or insculpted is not a natural kind but a social form (*vera haec conuigii forma*) amenable to the communication of a new form (*novam quamdam formam*) by the institution of the sacrament. (*Arcanum* §6, 13.)

43. "These parties, let it be noted, not fettered but adorned by the golden bond of the sacrament, not hampered but assisted, should strive with all their might to the end that their wedlock, not only through the power and symbolism of the sacrament, but also through their spirit and manner of life, may be and remain always the living image [*viva imago*] of that most fruitful union of Christ with the Church, which is to be venerated as the sacred token of most perfect love.... [Christ] desired marriage to be and made it the mystical image of His own ineffable union with the Church [*qui matrimonium mysticuam esse voluit effecitque imaginem suae ineffabilis cum ecclesia coniunctionis*]." Here, splicing together *Casti* §§42, 129.

44. *Casti* §29.

the dignity of *imago*. And not just any sacral image, but from a theological standpoint, a plutonium-grade image: namely, *imago Christi*. The "whole Christ" who not only incorporates human nature body and soul, but also concorporates, which is to say, he founds a social body which is the *Christus totus*.[45] We have, in short, an image derived not just from afar, in the processions of the divine persons, but one more immediately in the mission of the incarnate second person. Here, there is a new and distinct ground for affirming *unto the image and likeness*. If we apply the three aspects of Eucharist to marriage, we identify the *sacramentum tantum*, the sign alone, which is a conjugal union of man and woman; the *sacramentum et res,* the sign together with its internal reality, the union of Christ and the church; and the *res tantum,* communion in a social unity of order.

Even so, it depends in part upon the integrity of the natural sign, which is marriage itself. This is why the legal, political, and philosophical conflict between the modern state and the church over marriage and divorce was intimately related to both social doctrine and to sacramental theology. Sacramental marriage was the test case for things that are both higher and lower than the state. Marriage is a social entity that not only fits the Dionysian formula, but enjoys a special status. Although it is in one sense lower than the state, in another sense it is, as Pius asserted, more sacred than the state. For its social form is not only directly instituted by God, but is also the natural sign of Christ's social body. Here, the social form is called *imago*—the *conformatio* of spouses is a sign of Christ, whose incarnation is not merely an *incorporatio* (God taken flesh) but also a *concorporatio,* the establishment by grace of a social body. This social body is, in the strict sense of the term, *imago Christi*.

45. CCC 794–95.

ECCLESIOLOGICAL THEMES

In the opening pages of *Lumen gentium,* the Second Vatican Council's constitution on the church, we read that the ecclesial union is "like a sacrament."[46] In fact, the idea that the church is in some analogous way a sacramental image is presented so quickly that one might think that it is either a pure assertion or that the argument had already been made. Indeed, it had been made in Pius XII's *Mystici corporis.* Writing in 1943, in the middle of World War II, Pius set out to explain why the primary mission of the church is to be Christ's social body, and thereby to be the eschatological sign of the unity of the human race.

In *Mystici,* Pius gives a rather thorough survey of the different ways that a social unity transcends the sum of its parts without destruction of its individual members. The church, he notes, shares many of these predicates: it is a unity of order that does not destroy its individual members, it enjoys an intrinsic common good, functional organicity, and so forth. Unlike other societies, however, the mystical body of Christ has no identity other than being Christ's social body. In the case of marriage we can speak of a natural form that achieves a higher unity by the habilitation of grace. For its part, the church has no identity other than being grafted onto and conformed to its Head. It has no form other than

46. "Since the Church is in Christ like a sacrament or as a sign and instrument both of a very closely knit union with God and of the unity of the whole human race" (§1). Constituted and ordered "as a society" (§8), the church includes what is "suitable for visible and social unity"—a "visible sacrament of this saving unity." For John Paul II's account of the analogous uses of sacrament, see "Man in the Dimension of Gift," general audience of February 29, 1980, in *Man and Woman He Created Them,* at 203. The reader should note that John Paul II uses the words sign and sacrament in analogous ways; see also "Marriage as Figure and as Sacrament of the New Covenant," general audience of October 20, 1982, ibid. at 510–12. On his understanding of restricted and wide senses of sacrament, consult the useful index by Michael Waldstein.

the actions of its members through the outpouring of charity, the ordering of the Holy Spirit, and sacramental actions. Were the church only a social and juridical unity, it would be a social entity of some sort (like a club, or association), but it would not be the church, even if it still shows up in the Yellow Pages.

Pius writes that, by sanctifying grace, we are conformed to the image of the Son of God, and renewed according to the image of him who created us.[47] But he goes on to argue, "It is the will of Jesus Christ that the whole body of the Church, no less than the individual members, should resemble Him."[48] Precisely as a society, the church is Christ's social body expressing "both exterior and interior, a most faithful image of Christ."[49] Citing Bellarmine and Gregory of Nyssa, Pius insists that the Church is a *person*, called Christ.[50] The whole Christ (*Christum totum*) is the head and his social body.[51]

The surprising thing at Vatican II was not *Lumen gentium,* which completed Pius's encyclical on the church as social *imago Christi.* Rather, the surprising issue was tucked inside of *Gaudium et spes,* where the council treats the (natural) dignity of the individual as *imago Dei.* Early drafts had emphasized Genesis 1:17, "male and female he created them."[52] Rightly so, for traditionally

47. *Mystici corporis: imagini Filii dei,* citing Rom 8:29, Col 3:10, §46.

48. Ibid., §47.

49. Ibid., §48; *Christi imaginem quam perfectissime exprimat,* ibid., §54.

50. Ibid., §53. *Ut ipsa quasi altera Christi persona existat*—"the social Body of the Church [*sociale Ecclesiae Corpus*] should be honored by the name of Christ—namely, that our Savior Himself sustains in a divine manner the society which He founded." §52.

51. "Herein we find the reason why, according to the opinion of Augustine already referred to, the mystical Head, which is Christ, and the Church, which here below as another Christ shows forth His person, constitute one new man, in whom heaven and earth are joined together in perpetuating the saving work of the Cross: Christ We mean, the Head and the Body, the whole Christ." Ibid., §77

52. My account of the discussion at Vatican II and its implications for the work

that scriptural verse was referenced for the estate of marriage in the beginning (Mt 19), Christ's prayer for the unity of the church (Jn 17), and the Pauline teaching about the "great sacrament" of Christ and his church (Eph 5). All these scriptural passages suppose that a social union is a sign of the sacred. And while the signs differ according to sacramental economies (creation and redemption), the primordial analogue of the human person made unto the image and likeness of God, male and female, is rather important. It stands prominently in both creation and redemption.

At the council, some bishops wanted to say that the social relation is, by creation and not just by grace, a fundamental aspect \ of the *imago*. Other bishops, however, worried that if the *imago* is predicated on the relation it would imply that the human person receives the *imago* from a relation to others (*ex relatione ad alios*).[53] This would not only stumble into the heresy that holds that the *imago* is assembled through social relationships; it would also mislead and derogate from the dignity of the individual, under attack in modern times. We recall that in 1965 the totalitarian regimes were still in place. So, they compromised. Here's how the relevant section of *Gaudium et spes* §24 reads in its final form:

> Indeed, the Lord Jesus, when He prayed to the Father, "that all may be one ... as we are one" [John 17:21–22] opened up vistas closed to human reason, for He implied a certain likeness between the union of the divine Persons, and the unity of God's sons in truth and charity. This likeness [*similitudo*] reveals that man, who is the only creature on earth which God willed for itself, cannot fully find himself except through a sincere gift of himself.

---

of John Paul II is indebted to the work of Jaroslav Kupchek, O.P. "Komunijny wymiar obrazu Bożego w człowieku w soborowej konstytucji Gaudium et spes," *Studia Theologica Varsaviensia* 44 (2006), 1, s. 139–58. His full work is his book on John Paul II's theology of *imago Dei: Dar i komunia. Teologia ciała w ujęciu Jana Pawła II* (Kraków, 2006), s. 199–241.

    53. *Acta Synodolia*—AS 1, 4a, s. 720.

The council took from *Casti connubii* Pius XI's description of the matrimonial society as a "sincere gift" and then spliced it together with Christ's prayer for the church's union in the order of grace. Interestingly, rather than dealing straight on with the question of the natural condition of the *imago* in the order of creation, they quote authoritative texts which pertain to how, in the order of grace, matrimony and church are *imagines Christi*. Although the text clearly indicates a natural law position when it proposes that man is perfected by making a sincere gift of himself, the authoritative sources for the social aspects are taken from the New Covenant without the natural fundament drawn from Genesis. Leaving out Genesis, and moving directly to John 17, it seems that the social aspect of the image of God is constituted entirely by grace, which of course is not quite right on the traditional reading of Genesis 1:26 and Ephesians 5.

JOHN PAUL II AND THE THEOLOGY
OF THE BODY

Upon his election in 1978, John Paul II began to rework *Gaudium et spes* §24. "The Second Vatican Council, in speaking of the likeness of God, uses extremely significant terms," he noted. "It refers not only to the divine image and likeness which every human being as such already possesses, but also and primarily [*verum etiam et praesertim*] to a certain similarity between the union of the divine persons and the union of God's children in truth and love."[54]

In his lengthy series of Wednesday audiences, the pope argued that Adam's solitude, mythically represented in Genesis 2, confirms the notion that the individual person is the bearer of a divine-like dignity. Everything in the solitude, the pope insists,

54. Letter to Families, §8.

must be affirmed as that which constitutes *man*.[55] In other words, Adamic solitude represents what the tradition meant by substantial unity—a perfection that cannot be supplanted or canceled by social relations. In origin, form, and finality the individual is created for God alone, and thus is said to be made unto the image of God. In Genesis, of course, Adamic solitude is resolved by God, who puts Adam into a sleep, from which the original Adam awakes, male and female. Adam's solitude is addressed not by assimilation to another natural substance, nor by the creation of a new substance, but by a *communio personarum*—a sexually differentiated community of persons.

What's important, for our purposes, is John Paul's conclusion to this line of thought:

If … we want to retrieve also from the account of the Yahwist text the concept of "image of God," we can deduce that *man became the image of God not only through his own humanity, but also through the communion of persons,* which man and woman form from the very beginning. The function of the image is that of mirroring the one who is the model, of reproducing its own prototype. Man becomes an image of God not so much in the moment of solitude as in the moment of communion. He is, in fact, "from the beginning" not only an image in which the solitude of one Person, who rules the world, mirrors itself, but also and essentially the image of an inscrutable divine communion of Persons.[56]

Right away we should put aside the idea that the pope means chronological moments. The preceding discussion of Adamic solitude makes clear enough that the created image is not being assembled in time or constituted by adding sociological relations. Perhaps we can interpret the passage as an exegetical deepening

55. John Paul II, "The Meaning of Original Unity," general audience of November 14, 1979, in *Man and Woman He Created Them,* at 162.
56. Ibid., at 163.

of the Dionysian formula of a double imitation: first, the moment of solitude representing the image vested in the substantial nature, and second the gift and communion, representing diffusion of the good. The individual is perfected as a member in union with others by performing acts of giving and receiving, and in this sense "becomes" the image in its perfection. Hence, both the image and its *similitudo*. In fact, John Paul elsewhere refers explicitly to the Dionysian principle in what he calls the double subjectivity of the *imago*.[57] The human creature, he says, images the Trinity in his own subjectivity and as a member of a social subjectivity—it is in the nature of the created *imago* to diffuse the good through reciprocity of the gift.

There is no question but that he wants to enrich the primordial sign or the sacramentality of the *humanum* precisely in its "unity of the two."[58] For the Catholic tradition, sacramental theology (of marriage) and ecclesiology require this union, "from the beginning." The pope asserts a relational ontology of the created *imago* that *Gaudium et spes* §24 hesitated to affirm.

57. "There is a shortage of people with whom to create and share the common good; and yet that good, by its nature, demands to be created and shared with others, *bonum est diffusivum sui:*'good is diffusive of itself.' The more 'common' the good, the 'more properly one's own' it will also be: mine—yours—ours. This is the logic behind living according to the good, living in truth and charity. If man is able to accept and follow this logic, his life truly becomes a 'sincere gift'" (*donum sincerum*). Letter to Families §10. He is referring here to *Gaudium et spes* §24.

58. "The fundamental reason [*fundamentalis ratio*] that requires and explains the presence and the collaboration of both men and women is not only, as it was just emphasized, the major source of meaning and efficacy in the pastoral action of the Church, nor *even less is it the simple sociological fact* of sharing a life together as human beings, which is natural for man and woman. It is, rather, the original plan of the Creator who from the 'beginning' willed the human being to be a 'unity of the two,' and willed man and woman to be the prime community of persons, source of every other community, and, at the same time, to be a 'sign' of that interpersonal communion of love which constitutes the mystical, intimate life of God, One in Three." *Solicitudo rei socialis*, §52.

⟍ Thus, in this dimension, a primordial *sacrament* is constituted, understood as a sign that efficaciously transmits in the visible world the invisible mystery hidden in God from eternity. The sacrament, as a visible sign, is constituted with man, inasmuch as he is a "body," through his "visible" masculinity and femininity. The body, in fact, and only the body, is capable of making visible what is invisible: the spiritual and the divine. It has been created to transfer into the visible reality of the world the mystery hidden from eternity in God, and thus to be a sign of it.[59]

The International Theological Commission for two years studied these issues, and in 2003 submitted to Cardinal Ratzinger, president of the commission, a document entitled *Communion and Stewardship: Human Persons Created in the Image of God.* Referring to Genesis 1:26, the commission states: "God placed the first human beings in relation to one another, each with a partner of the other sex.... According to this conception, man is not an isolated individual but a person—an essentially relational being.... The fundamentally relational character of the *imago Dei* itself constitutes its ontological structure."[60] The relational nature, they say, "belongs to the specific manner in which the *imago Dei* exists."[61] The commission rejected any sort of dualism that would vest the image only in the psychological capacities to the exclusion of the human body; and it denied any sort of monism that would vest the image only in the actualization of the individual.[62] This language,

59. General audience of February 20, 1980, in *Man and Woman He Created Them,* at 203. Again, for his understanding of restricted and wide senses of sacrament, see the index by Michael Waldstein.

60. *Communion and Stewardship,* §10.

61. Ibid., §33. This proposition should be interpreted in the fashion of Thomas (De Ver. 21.5), namely that the created human being is not good in every respect it needs to be good without the proper complement of accidents, for example, habits and relations.

62. "Two themes converge to shape the biblical perspective. In the first place,

however, presupposes a distinction between substance and relation so that the latter can truly represent a perfection of the former.

The commission therefore pursued the stronger and broader interpretation of the Trinitarian and relational structure of the created *imago*. It also emphasized the sacramental context of *imago Christi:* "The created image affirmed by the Old Testament is, according to the New Testament, to be completed in the *imago Christi*. In the New Testament development of this theme, two distinctive elements emerge: the Christological and Trinitarian character of the *imago Dei,* and the role of sacramental mediation in the formation of the *imago Christi.*"[63] Not surprisingly, marriage is taken to be the chief instance of both the natural and supernaturally elevated situation of the *imago*. Marriage is the foundational example for both the natural and supernatural social principles of man being made unto the image and likeness of God.

the whole of man is seen as created in the image of God. This perspective excludes interpretations which locate the *imago Dei* in one or another aspect of human nature (for example, his upright stature or his intellect) or in one of his qualities or functions (for example, his sexual nature or his domination of the earth). Avoiding both monism and dualism, the Bible presents a vision of the human being in which the spiritual is understood to be a dimension together with the physical, social and historical dimensions of man" *Communion and Stewardship,* §9. Later, the document notes: "Present-day theology is striving to overcome the influence of dualistic anthropologies that locate the *imago Dei* exclusively with reference to the spiritual aspect of human nature. Partly under the influence first of Platonic and later of Cartesian dualistic anthropologies, Christian theology itself tended to identify the *imago Dei* in human beings with what is the most specific characteristic of human nature, viz., mind or spirit. The recovery both of elements of biblical anthropology and of aspects of the Thomistic synthesis has contributed to the effort in important ways." §27. The Thomistic synthesis, meaning hylemorphism, the soul as the form of the body. Thomas held that although the created *imago* is chiefly the soul, it also applies to the human body insofar as the rational soul is its "form." See *Super Sent.,* lib. 3 d. 2 q. 1 a. 3 qc. 1 ad 2, where he contends that the living body is *similitudo imaginii.* Also, see his interesting but rather brief thoughts on the comparison of the imprinted *imago* respectively in the angelic and human beings for whom corporeality adds a good that is specific to the human *imago,* in S.t. I 93.3.

63. *Communion and Stewardship,* §11.

While it is certainly true that union between human beings can be realized in a variety of ways, Catholic theology today affirms that marriage constitutes an elevated form of the communion between human persons and one of the best analogies of the Trinitarian life. When a man and a woman unite their bodies and spirits in an attitude of total openness and self-giving, they form *a new image of God.* Their union as one flesh does not correspond simply to a biological necessity, but to the intention of the Creator in leading them to share the happiness of being made in his image. The Christian tradition speaks of marriage as an eminent way of sanctity.[64]

CONCLUSION

Benedict XVI's first encyclical, *Deus caritas est* (2005), immediately picks up this theme of image and union of persons. The biblical faith shows something new about God and man. God is revealed as capable of a unity of love with the creature "in which both God and man remain themselves and yet become fully one."[65] God not only creates and capacitates the human being, but initiates a society with man. On the anthropological side, the solitude of Adam can be contrasted with the Platonic myth in the *Symposium,* according to which the original *humanum* is a self-sufficient sphere, who, for the sake of punishment, is broken into two. In the Platonic myth, the loss of original self-sufficiency and the ensuing quest for relationship is a penal exercise; in Genesis 2

---

64. Ibid., §38 (emphasis added). And beyond marriage, to the race: "Every individual human being as well as the whole human community are created in the image of God. In its original unity—of which Adam is the symbol—the human race is made in the image of the divine Trinity. Willed by God, it makes its way through the vicissitudes of human history towards a perfect communion, also willed by God, but yet to be fully realized. In this sense, human beings share the solidarity of a unity that both already exists and is still to be attained." §43.

65. *Deus caritas est,* §10.

the communion of Adam and Eve represent a completion in one flesh.[66] Hence, the society is not a diremption but a fulfillment of individual's humanity.

Because the social principle is woven into the deepest mysteries of God and man, Christianity can be said to be a "sacramental mysticism [that] is social in character."[67] It is a doctrine of communion. Properly understood, in charity "the usual contraposition between worship and ethics simply falls apart."[68] Eucharist is ⟋ communion with God and neighbor, which is the essence of the two great commandments. In his subsequent encyclical, *Spe salvi* (2007), Benedict insists along this same line of thought that individualism obscures the Christian understanding of salvation as a social reality.[69] Here, the pope cites Henri de Lubac, who contended in *Catholicisme: les aspects sociaux du dogme* (Catholicism: The Social Aspects of Doctrine) that the church's social teachings are nothing less than the church's self-understanding of the mystery of ecclesial communion. "It is social," he explained, "in the deepest sense of the word: not merely in its applications in the field of natural institutions but first and foremost in itself, in the heart of its mystery, in the essence of its dogma. It is social in a sense which should have made the expression 'social Catholicism' pleonastic."[70] Interestingly, when he was cardinal prefect of the Congregation for the Doctrine of the Faith, Joseph Ratzinger wrote a new foreword to de Lubac's treatise, noting: "The social dimension which de Lubac saw rooted in deepest mystery has often sunk to the merely sociological so that the unique Christian contribution

---

66. Ibid., §11.

67. Ibid., §14.

68. Ibid.

69. *Spe salvi*, §14.

70. English translation, *Catholicism: Christianity and the Common Destiny of Man*, trans. Lancelot C. Sheppard and Sister Elizabeth Englund, O.C.D., the most recent edition with a foreword by Joseph Cardinal Ratzinger (San Francisco: Ignatius Press, 1988), at 15.

to the right understanding of history and community has disappeared from sight. Instead of a leaven for the age, or its salt, we are often simply its echo."

The mission of the church is to be the sacrament of *concorporatio*, that is, Christ taking a social body that images the communion of divine persons.[71] In this, Benedict echoes the *Catechism of the Catholic Church:* "The vocation of humanity is to show forth the image of God and to be transformed into the image of the Father's only Son."[72] An adequate anthropology must include, without confusion or reduction, the two memberships—the individual as human person, and as a member of social orders. Both are manifest in the economies of creation and redemption. Individualism not only occludes the dignity of membership in society, but also presents a distorted understanding of the individual.

At the outset I pointed out that the human *imago Dei* as a created analogue of a Trinity of divine persons is in the public domain only by virtue of revelation. Given the ecumenical scope of this book, and echoing here a point made by Father John Behr, Christians of all stripes constantly need to be reminded that not every dignitarian proposition is the same as the revealed truth that man is made unto the image and likeness of God. The teaching of Genesis and the New Testament about the created and transformed image is not a bottom-drawer garment covering Christian theology and the various humanisms.[73] The same thing must be said for the social and sacramental aspect of the image in the case of marriage and the church. All of this is something more than a merely "adequate anthropology." It is "adequate" to what Scripture and tradition teach about the whole truth.

71. *Caritas in veritate*, §54.   72. CCC §1877.

73. As Benedict XVI says in *Deus caritas est* (§18), "If I have no contact whatsoever with God in my life, then I cannot see in the other anything more than the other, and I am incapable of seeing in him the image of God."

Theological anthropology, however, includes common experience and those truths which can be gathered from it. Two seem to be of special importance. First, that the human person possesses a unity of being and operation that manifests certain excellences. This kind of dignity is in the public domain by common experience. Indeed, many wisdom traditions have taken note of the divine-like human capacities. Second, that there is a real and not merely a nominal difference between aggregations of human persons and social unions. The distinction comes from Aristotle, and it hardly depends upon special revelation. These two—the excellence of the human person and the excellence of social unions—are, so to speak, "preambles" of the theology of the image of God. In the modern era, faced with liberal individualism and various statist ideologies of collectivism, the church has had to make even more clear the two anthropological aspects of the created image.

These and other natural fundaments are not simply a question of apologetics but a question of the coherence of theology. Even if in a certain place and time a culture should obscure these preambles, and even if philosophical, political, and legal debates about the most fundamental aspects of the human being prove intractable, it would not imply that we can ignore the natural estate of the human person by moving to theological anthropology. For revelation itself will not allow us to remain silent about the preambles. As Jesus said about divorce, "In the beginning it was not so." Marriage in the economy of redemption presupposes marriage, however broken the institution might be in a particular society. The ecclesiology of the Mystical Body presupposes a social unity not reducible to aggregated individuals. In sum, the social aspects of *imago Dei* and *imago Christi* would remain a crucial theme in theology simply on its own terms. Surely, this is what de Lubac meant when he asserted that Catholic theology "is social in a sense which should have made the expression 'social Catholicism' pleonastic."

[3]

THE AUDACITY
OF THE *IMAGO DEI*

THE LEGACY AND UNCERTAIN FUTURE
OF HUMAN DIGNITY

C. BEN MITCHELL

WHAT does it mean to be human?[1] What does it mean to be "one of us"? The emerging revolution in biotechnology challenges us to redefine human nature for the sake of technological development.

1. A host of conferences and books have examined this question during the past decade or so. Provocative titles include: Warren S. Brown, Nancey Murphy, and H. Newton Malony, eds., *Whatever Happened to the Soul? Scientific and Theological Portraits of Human Nature* (Minneapolis: Fortress Press, 1998); Jean Bethke Elshtain, *Who Are We? Critical Reflections and Hopeful Possibilities* (Grand Rapids, Mich.: Eerdmans, 2000); John F. Kavanaugh, *Who Count as Persons? Human Identity and the Ethics of Killing* (Washington, D.C.: Georgetown University Press, 2001); and Harold W. Baillie and Timothy E. Casey, eds., *Is Human Nature Obsolete? Genetics, Bioengineering, and the Future of the Human Condition* (Cambridge, Mass.: MIT Press, 2005).

Advances in genetic engineering, pre-implantation genetic diagnosis, cybernetics, robotics, and nanotechnology depend in large measure on our willingness as a culture to recast what it means to be human. In ecumenical collaboration, Christians from all backgrounds ought to be invested in thinking through and thinking well about these issues.

Xenotransplantation and trans-species genetic engineering already have the potential to produce chimeras—living members of our species that share either discrete organs or some DNA from another species. Would an animal-human chimera be a member of our species? Would an animal-human chimera be a human person? Would the answer to that question depend on how many, or which, nonhuman organs were transplanted, or on what percentage of human DNA was retained? Should we define our humanity by the number and identity of our genes?

Alternatively, we might define what it means to be human as the possession of human consciousness. The mind, with its awareness of self and others, its perception of time and space, the presence of memory, and so on, might define human personhood. But, since many contemporary neuroscientists maintain that the mind is merely the complex interactions of the chemical processes of the brain, then what it means to be human would depend only on what is going on "in the head." But surely a human being is more than a brain in a vat.[2]

Will the present notion of what constitutes our humanity persevere throughout the century? Is there a truly human future? The Cambridge sociologist Margaret Archer once observed that "Modernity's 'Death of God' has now been matched by Postmodern-

---

2. This is an image borrowed from philosopher Hilary Putnam's famous thought experiment in *Reason, Truth, and History* (Cambridge: Cambridge University Press, 1982).

ism's 'Death of Humanity.'"[3] That is to say, as modernity was the age of philosophical deicide, postmodernity is the age of philosophical homicide. What role, if any, might a biblical-theological account of human nature and of humanity have in preserving human dignity against the challenges wrought by modernity and postmodernity, especially in their techno-utopian versions? Put differently, what does the ancient teaching of *imago Dei* have to say to a culture often enthralled by techno-socio-biological engineering in its efforts to produce a more fully evolved species— what some have called "the posthuman"?

But first, what might this "designer evolution" look like?[4] According to researchers such as the MIT robotics professor Rodney Brooks, through his own work Homo sapiens is evolving into a more perfect species, Robo sapiens. As a consequence, argues the journalist Robert Wright, this techno-evolution may mean that constitutional rights will have to be "recalibrated." "For all I know," he writes, "it's true that in 20 or 30 years these nanobots, by malicious design or by accident, will run so rampant that we'll be fondly reminiscing about the days of termites. On the other hand, this is basically the same problem that is posed by self-replicating biological agents (i.e., viruses). In both cases we're faced with microscopic things that can be inconspicuously made and transported and, once unleashed, whether intentionally or accidentally, can keep on truckin'."[5] Kevin Warwick of the University

3. Margaret S. Archer, *Being Human: The Problem of Agency* (Cambridge: Cambridge University Press, 2000), 1. Archer goes on to note that "now it is our job to reclaim Humanity which is indeed at risk. At least, it is at risk in the Academy, where strident voices would dissolve the human being into discursive structures and humankind into a disembodied textualism" (p. 2).

4. To borrow Simon Young's phrase in *Designer Evolution: A Transhumanist Manifesto* (New York: Prometheus Books, 2005).

5. Ibid., 30. See also Robert Wright, *The Moral Animal: The New Science of Evolutionary Psychology* (New York: Vintage, 1995).

of Reading believes that "the human race as we know it is very likely in its endgame."[6] According to Warwick, however, machines will not wipe out the human race, as sci-fi thrillers often suggest. Instead, by "grafting" human consciousness into extraordinarily fast, durable, and intelligent machines, *we will become them.* "*Homo sapiens* will vanish as a biological species, replacing itself with a new race of cyborgs."[7]

In her chronicle of our contemporary "robotic moment," social scientist Sherry Turkle suggests that "thinking about robots . . . is a way of thinking about the essence of personhood."[8] Turkle observes that our age of "technological promiscuity" is one in which "relationships with robots are ramping up; relationships with humans are ramping down."[9] As one thirty-year-old man told her in an interview, "I'd rather talk to a robot. Friends can be exhausting. The robot will always be there for me. And whenever I'm done, I can walk away."[10] Will we embrace robots as "human enough"? To some degree, are we doing this already?

According to other accounts the future may include human beings who transcend their biology. In fact, Ray Kurzweil, an award-winning inventor and futurist, is so bold as to maintain that "the singularity"—the culmination of our biological thinking and existence with our technology, "resulting in a world that is still human but transcends our biological roots"—will occur by the year 2045.[11]

6. Peter Menzel and Faith D'Aluisio, *Robo sapiens: Evolution of a New Species* (Cambridge, Mass.: MIT Press, 2000), 29.

7. Ibid., 31.

8. Sherry Turkle, *Alone Together: Why We Expect More from Technology and Less from Each Other* (New York: Basic Books, 2011), xvii.

9. Ibid., 19.

10. Ibid., 12.

11. Ray Kurzweil, *The Singularity Is Near: When Humans Transcend Biology* (New York: Viking, 2005).

The kind of moral quandaries I have cataloged led the President's Council on Bioethics to explore the idea and future of human dignity in its 2008 report, *Human Dignity and Bioethics*.[12] Will the notion of human dignity persist? What will be lost if it does not?

While some of these scenarios might seem far-fetched, prudence counsels that we take them seriously. Indeed, it is time that Christians put their divisions aside to think together about the challenges facing human dignity.

In what follows, I take stock of what the Christian Scriptures (where else would a Protestant start?!) and early tradition say about human dignity, before focusing on my own Protestant, and specifically Baptist, tradition. My hope is that scriptural hermeneutics and creedal and theological resources from Protestant traditions might help enrich all Christians desirous of thinking well about human dignity and its present-day challenges.

SCRIPTURE ON THE NATURE
OF HUMAN BEINGS

Then God said, "Let us make man in Our image, according to
our likeness. They will rule the fish of the sea, the birds of the sky,
the animals, all the earth, and the creatures that crawl on
the earth."

So God created man in His own image;
He created him in the image of God;
He created them male and female. (Gn 1:26–27)

The creation account in Genesis 1 and 2 uses the Hebrew noun *ādām* to describe both "humankind" and the individual person

---

12. *Human Dignity and Bioethics: Essays Commissioned by the President's Council on Bioethics* (Washington, D.C., 2008). Available at www.bioethics.gov.

named "Adam." When *ādām* is used with the definite article, typically the text is referring to "humankind" (as in Gn 1:27). When
the noun is used without the definite article, Adam, the man, is
usually in view.

＼ Human beings are *made* in the image of God (Gn 1:27). The
verb *bārā'* (to create) is used three times in Genesis 1 (vv. 1, 21, 27),
with the making of humanity as the zenith of God's creative activity. As Hans Walter Wolff nicely summarizes:

> [In Genesis] man's special position is no less clearly brought out. The ter-
> restrial animals, who are created immediately before man on the sixth
> day, proceed from the earth on the basis of a divine command to it; and
> God "makes them" [*'śh*] [vv. 24f.]. But the man and woman in Genesis
> 1 do not emerge from the depths of the earth; they are completely and
> independently created, without the materials being provided beforehand
> and without the co-operation of the earth (this is characterized by the
> threefold *br'* in v. 27), by God's own personal decision.... The blessing
> given to man in v. 28 differs fundamentally from that conferred on the
> fish and the birds in v. 22, in that after they are empowered to multiply,
> men are entrusted with lordship over the earth and especially over all
> animals (v. 28b). This defines the decisive difference between man and
> beast, and it again derives from God's relationship to man.[13]

We are told in Genesis 2 that God made the first man—similar to the other animals (cf. Gn 1:24)—from the "dust from the
ground," breathing "the breath of life into his nostrils" (Gn 2:7).
Thus, God made Adam a "living being" (*nepeš*). The material
of Adam's physical body was absolutely earthly (cf. Pss 90:3 and
103:14), the source of his life was definitely divine. Thus, humankind shares what H. D. McDonald calls "a mysterious bond so
that when man sinned the natural order was itself deeply afflicted

13. Hans Walter Wolff, *Anthropology of the Old Testament* (London: SCM Press,
1974), 95.

(Gen. 3:17–18; cf. Rom. 8:19–23)."[14] Nevertheless, humankind is presented throughout Scripture as distinct from the rest of creation.

As creatures, human beings belong to God in a special way. The Apostle Paul would later declare before the philosophers in Athens, "In [God] we live and move and exist, as even some of your own poets have said, 'For we are also His offspring'" (Acts 17:28). Creatureliness both elevates human beings (in that they are not accidents of history) and humbles them (because God is sovereign over them).

\ Despite the fact that all that God created conformed to his own purpose and will, and thus was "good," it was apparently not good for Adam to be alone (Gn 2:18). God made human beings sexual and relational creatures. Sexuality is both intrinsic to human nature and necessary for the perpetuation of the species. Even if we can admit that many gender distinctions are socially constructed, *that* human beings are gendered in the first place is a result of God's creational purpose.

Relationality is also an intrinsic feature of humanity. Adam's loneliness in the absence of a female partner suggests not merely the sexual but the social character of human beings. So for humankind's benefit, God graciously ordained that both human sexuality and sociability would find their fullest expression within the covenant of marriage where man and woman would enter a "one-flesh" relationship of unity for life (Gn 2:23–24).

But let me return to the notion of human beings cast in the *imago Dei*. As one of the leading evangelical theologians of the twentieth century, Carl F. H. Henry, once noted: "The importance of a proper understanding of the *imago Dei* can hardly be overstated.

14. H. D. McDonald, s.v. "Man, Doctrine of," in Walter A. Elwell, ed., *Evangelical Dictionary of Theology* (Carlisle, England: Paternoster, 1995).

The answer given to the *imago*-inquiry soon becomes determinative for the entire gamut of doctrinal affirmation. The ramifications are not only theological, but [for] every phase of the … cultural enterprise as a whole."[15] Henry was prescient. As we shall later see, the *imago Dei* has profound implications for understanding what a truly human future might look like. But even as we assert its importance, we can recognize that the doctrine only receives limited mention in Scripture. Still, as the University of Sheffield professor D. J. A. Clines keenly observes:

> The Old Testament references to the doctrine of the image of God in man are tantalizing in their brevity and scarcity; we find only the fundamental sentence in Genesis 1:26 "Let us make men in our image after our likeness," a further reference to man's creation "in the likeness of God" in Genesis 5:22, and a final statement in Genesis 9:6: "Whoever sheds the blood of man, by man shall his blood be shed; for God made man in his own image." Yet we become aware, in reading these early chapters of Genesis and in studying the history of the interpretation of these passages that the importance of the doctrine is out of all proportion to the laconic treatment it receives in the Old Testament.[16]

In Genesis 1, ' *ādām* is used generically for "humankind." The word is versatile in that it may refer to humankind, to an individual person (e.g., Gn 2:5, 7), or function as a proper name (e.g., Gn 5:1). Furthermore, we learn that humankind alone, among all created beings, is made in God's "image" (*tselem*) and "likeness" (*dĕmût*).

Tselem is also used in Genesis 9:6 and, in this context, highlights the distinction between humans and animals. While God gives to Noah and his progeny permission to kill animals for food,

---

15. Carl F. H. Henry, s.v. "Man," *Baker's Dictionary of Theology* (Grand Rapids, Mich.: Baker Book House, 1973).

16. D. J. A. Clines, "The Image of God in Man," *Tyndale Bulletin* 19 (1968): 53.

he declares: "Whoever sheds the blood of a human, by a human shall that person's blood be shed; for in his own image [*tselem*] God made humankind."[17] More importantly, this passage makes clear that God requires justice in relations between human beings. Interestingly, justice is grounded not only in the character of God, but in the character of his human creatures as imagers of God.

As the Baptist theologian James Leo Garrett points out, there are no other direct statements about the image of God in humankind in the rest of the Old Testament.[18] The apocryphal books, however, contain two significant passages that underscore the unique status of human beings: "For God created man to be immortal, and made him to be an image of his own eternity" (Wisdom of Solomon 2:23 AV) and "He [the Lord] endued them with strength by themselves, and made them according to his image, and put the fear of man upon all flesh, and gave him dominion over the beasts and fowls" (Ecclesiasticus 17:3-4 AV).

In the New Testament, two nouns are used for the image of God. *Eikōn* ("image") is found in four Pauline letters with respect to the image of God in humankind: 1 Corinthians 11:7; 2 Corinthians 3:18; Romans 8:29; and Colossians 3:9-10. The other noun, *homoiōsis* ("likeness"), is found only in James 3:9.

17. Paul K. Jewett points out that "the reason why the concept of the divine image has become so prominent in Christian anthropology is obvious: it confers on the human subject the highest possible distinction, leaving the world of animals far behind. Here is language used of no other creature, language that teaches us to understand ourselves in terms of God rather than in terms of the animals. While we share with them a common mortality in the flesh, the Creator has endowed us with uncommon gifts in the spirit. Our mammalian ancestry, whatever it may be, is therefore a matter essentially indifferent so far as a Christian understanding of humankind is concerned. In other words, Christian anthropology is done from above, not from below." Paul K. Jewett with Marguerite Shuster, *Who We Are: Our Dignity as Human* (Grand Rapids, Mich.: Eerdmans, 1996), 54.

18. James Leo Garrett, *Systematic Theology: Biblical, Historical, and Theological*, vol. 1 (Grand Rapids, Mich.: Eerdmans, 1990), 392.

\ Curiously, nowhere does Scripture tell us precisely in what the image of God consists. Biblical commentators and theologians, however, have not shied away from speculating. Garrett observes, for instance, that theological interpretations of the *imago Dei* have included (1) humankind's erect bodily form, (2) human dominion over nature, (3) human reason, (4) human prelapsarian righteousness, (5) human capacities, (6) the juxtaposition between man and woman, (7) responsible creaturehood and moral conformity to God, and (8) some composite view.[19] The systematic theologian Millard Erickson treats three general views of the *imago Dei* that he categorizes as substantive, relational, and functional.[20] And the Australian Anglican theologian Charles Sherlock notes that the image of God in humankind at a minimum must involve "relationships with God, one another, and creation."[21]

The literature on this subject is indeed large, but I think it fair to recognize two dominant categories of interpretation: substantialism and relationalism.[22] Substantialists typically identify that which makes us human as some immaterial aspect of our humanity. For instance, many of the early Fathers of the Church, and later Thomas Aquinas, believed that human rationality constituted the sine qua non of our humanity. This view doubtlessly owes a significant debt to the classical philosophical tradition in general and to Plato and Aristotle in particular. By contrast, relationalists are more inclined to locate human uniqueness in humanity's special relationship with God. These would include many in the

19. Ibid., 394–403.

20. Millard J. Erickson, *Christian Theology*, unabridged one-volume edition (Grand Rapids, Mich.: Baker Book House, 1986), 498–517.

21. Charles Sherlock, *The Doctrine of Humanity* (Downers Grove, Ill.: InterVarsity Press, 1996), 73.

22. For instance, see F. W. Bridger, s.v. "Humanity," in David J. Atkinson, David F. Field, Arthur Holmes, and Oliver O'Donovan, eds., *New Dictionary of Christian Ethics and Pastoral Theology* (Downers Grove, Ill.: InterVarsity Press, 1995).

Reformed tradition, such as Calvin and Barth. Sometimes relationalists have appealed to the doctrine of the Trinity as a paradigm for the divine/human relationship. Stanley Rudman raises an important caution about this way of understanding relationality, however. "The doctrine of the Trinity," he writes," is not part of a campaign to improve human relationships."[23] That is to say, our understanding of Trinitarian relationality should not be psychologized in order to explain our humanity because (1) the fundamental differences between God as Creator and human beings as created should not be blurred and (2) direct inferences between inter-Trinitarian life and human relationships are unwarranted because of the sui generis nature of the Godhead.

D. J. A. Clines persuasively argues that Genesis 1:26 is sometimes mistranslated. The most natural meaning of the Hebrew phrase םיהלא םלצב (in the image of God) "is that God has an image, and that man is created in conformity with this image."[24] In this case, the Hebrew prepositional prefix ב (*beth*) signifies conforming to a norm. The word would be translated, "according to the pattern, or model, of our image." This interpretation raises a question, however. From the point of view of ancient Near Eastern thought, argues Clines, such an image would be conceived of as either a physical form or a spiritual quality or character. Despite the numerous anthropomorphisms used to describe God and God's activity, and despite his appearances in theophanies, Scripture appears to maintain that, apart from the Incarnation of Christ, God is emphatically *not* a physical being.[25]

Moreover, Clines argues, the ב should not be taken as the *beth* of a norm, meaning that the image should be understood meta-

---

23. Stanley Rudman, *Concepts of Persons and Christian Ethics* (Cambridge: Cambridge University Press, 1997), 172.

24. Clines, "The Image of God in Man," 70.

25. Ibid., 72.

phorically, referring to some quality or characteristic of the divine nature in the pattern of which humanity is made. There are only two passages in which the word *tselem* (image) might be used in this way (Pss 39:6; 73:20). Yet in both cases, the idea of shape, form, or figure is still prominent. Thus, writes Clines, "no example remotely matches the meaning צלם would have in Genesis 1:26 if it referred to God's spiritual qualities or character, according to the pattern of which man has been made."[26]

A much more satisfactory way of rendering *tselem* with the *beth* here is the *beth* of essence, meaning "as" or "in the capacity of." The classic example, according to Clines, is Exodus 6:3 where God tells Moses: "I appeared to Abraham, Isaac, and Jacob *as* God Almighty." That is, God appeared *in the capacity or nature as* El Shaddai'. Following a considerable engagement with objections to taking Genesis 1:26 as a *beth* of essence, Clines concludes that "Genesis 1:26 ought to be translated 'Let us make man as our image' or 'to be our image,' and the other references to the image are to be interpreted similarly. Thus we may say that according to Genesis 1, man does not have the image of God, nor is he made *in* the image of God, but man is himself the image of God."[27] Clines's conclusion is especially helpful for its clarity, so allow me quote him at length:

Man is created not in God's image, since God has no image of His own, but as God's image, or rather to be God's image, that is to deputize [man] in the created world for the transcendent God who remains outside the world order. That man is God's image means that he is the visible corporeal representative of the invisible, bodiless God; he is representative rather than representation, since the idea of portrayal is secondary in the significance of the image. However, the term "likeness" is an assurance that man

26. "Ibid., 75.
27. Ibid., 80.

is an adequate and faithful representative of God on earth. The whole man is the image of God, without distinction of spirit and body. All mankind, without distinction, are the image of God. The image is to be understood not so much ontologically as existentially: it comes to expression not in the nature of man so much as in his activity and function. This function is to represent God's lordship to the lower orders of creation. The dominion of man over creation can hardly be excluded from the content of the image itself. Mankind, which means both the human race and individual men, do not cease to be the image of God so long as they remain men; to be human and to be the image of God are not separable.[28]

＼ Several important ideas follow from this discussion of the *imago Dei* helpful for a Christian anthropology. First, human beings were made by the special creative act of a sovereign God. Like all other aspects of God's creation, human beings, therefore, have been created with a telos, a purpose, to conform to the will of a good and gracious Creator. Second, all human beings—all members of the species Homo sapiens—are imagers of God. Every human being is, therefore, to be respected and every human life is to be viewed as possessing special dignity. Variability with respect to age, intellectual capacity, physical ability, ethnicity, etc., does not result in any diminution of the divine image, since all members of the species are imagers of God.[29] Third, insofar as he or she is able to fulfill them, certain privileges and responsibilities belong to every imager of God, including the responsibility to obey the creational mandate to procreate fruitfully and to steward the earth responsibly (Gn 1:28). As revelation unfolds, we understand that human beings are social, relational, reproductive, and responsible. Fourth, since the image is not reducible to a set of functional ca-

28. Ibid., 101.
29. See my essay "The Vulnerable—Abortion and Disability," in Gerald R. McDermott, ed., *The Oxford Handbook of Evangelical Theology* (Oxford: Oxford University Press, 2010), 481–96.

pacities, something human beings do, but a status human beings possess—who they are—then the image is *not* something human beings lose as a result of sin. (Some have mistakenly charged Protestants of holding this view.) In fact, well after the story of the fall of humankind, Genesis 9:1–6 reminds us that the reason homicide is so detestable to God is because killing another human being is destroying an imager of God.

Finally, we must ask, what is the relationship of the various aspects of our humanity (body, soul, will, etc.) to our being imagers of God? This leads to the question of whether human beings are holistic creatures or whether they should be viewed as dualistic beings. "Most commentators," observes Kenneth Matthews, "have anatomized the individual person into material and spiritual properties, thus identifying the imago Dei as either physical or spiritual. This dichotomy, however, is at odds with Hebrew anthropology; as [Genesis] 2:7 bears out, a person is viewed as a unified whole. The whole person, even all human life collectively, is in mind in [Genesis] 1:26."[30] We would do well then not to locate the *imago Dei* in some component of our identity, but in the created whole.

IMAGO DEI IN PROTESTANT PERSPECTIVE

Although proponents of *sola Scriptura,* the early Reformers, we must remember, placed considerable stock in the early ecumenical creeds of the church.[31] So before turning to Protestantism per se, a brief stop at the early church is warranted. As things stand, however, early creeds do not offer a fully developed anthropology.

30. Kenneth A. Matthews, *Genesis 1–11:26, The New American Commentary,* vol. 1A (Nashville, Tenn.: Broadman & Holman Publishers, 1996), 167–68.

31. On this point, see Carl E. Braaten and Robert W. Jenson, eds., *The Catholicity of the Reformation* (Grand Rapids, Mich.: Eerdmans, 1996).

For instance, the Apostles' Creed, recited in many Protestant denominations today, contains no explicit anthropological reference, with the exception that the creed affirms the bodily resurrection and human immortality: "I believe in ... the resurrection of the body; and the life everlasting."[32] Similarly, with respect to humankind, the Nicene Creed (A.D. 325) affirms only that "we look for the resurrection of the dead; and the life of the world to come." Although the burden of the ecumenical creeds was not anthropology per se, the Christological affirmations of early orthodoxy did have (and continue to have) significant implications for anthropology.

Commenting on the contribution of the early church, the historian Gary B. Ferngren has shown that among the non-Christian classical Greek and Roman writers, the ascription of dignity or human worth was reserved only for virtuous persons. "Human worth ... was not regarded in the classical world as intrinsic."[33] Nor were human rights intrinsic. They were defined juridically based on social, familial, or class membership. Slaves, foreigners, and foundlings might be granted certain privileges, but they were not regarded as rights holders. In Ferngren's words:

There was ... little sympathy in early Greek literature for the physically impaired or oppressed, an attitude that can be demonstrated to have characterized both popular and official opinion in virtually every period of classical antiquity. Attitudes to the physically defective reflected the belief that health and physical wholeness were essential to human dignity, so much so that life without them was not thought to be worth living. Citizenship, kinship, status, merit, and virtue formed the foundation of claims to the possession of human rights or human worth. Those who lacked them (e.g., orphans, slaves, foundlings, the physically defective,

32. Phillip Schaff, *The Creeds of Christendom: With a History and Critical Notes,* vol. 1, 6th ed., 1931 (Grand Rapids, Mich.: Baker Book House, 1985), 21–22.

33. Gary B. Ferngren, *Medicine and Health Care in Early Christianity* (Baltimore: Johns Hopkins University Press, 2009), 95.

prisoners) had no claim to the rights that they alone guaranteed or even to a recognition of their human worth.[34]

In contrast, early Jewish and Christian views of human worth were shaped by the theological notion that all human beings were created in the image of God. For Christians, moreover, the worth of human life was amplified through the Incarnation, since through it God sacralized human nature, as it were. Being both divine and human, Jesus demonstrated that embodied human nature was not to be despised as evil, but embraced as worthy of divine redemption.

As Ferngren points out, teachings on the *imago Dei* were formative in shaping Christian views of humanity, ethics, and ministry. First, the doctrine gave impetus to Christian charity and philanthropy. Just as concern for the lowly and poor had been an abiding feature of the Hebrew Scriptures, so charity and compassion were regarded as manifestations of Christian love (*agape*) and devotion to Christ. God's love for human beings was to be imitated by extending love to a brother or sister made in the image of God (Jn 13:34–35). Religion that is pure and undefiled before God was defined, at least partially, as caring for "orphans and widows in their distress" (Jas 1:27), two classes of vulnerable people.

Second, the doctrine of the image of God provided the ground for the belief that every human life possesses intrinsic value as a bearer of God's image and the object of redemption through Christ. This contrasted sharply with a number of ideas and practices in the ancient world and formed the principle behind early Christian repudiation of abortion, infanticide, gladiatorial games, and suicide.

Third, Christian understanding of the *imago Dei* gave Christians a new perception of embodiment and human personality.

34. Ibid., 95–96.

Greek ascetics, and later various Neoplatonic and Gnostic groups, had little admiration or concern for the body. On the contrary, they often despised it and looked forward to the day when they would be released from its prison house. The image of God, especially as reflected and amplified in the Incarnation, gave rise to notions of a more integrated body and soul, with Christ himself being the exemplar. "The Christian conception of Jesus as perfect man contributed," Ferngren avers, "to raising the body to a status that it had never enjoyed in paganism."[35]

Finally, the doctrine of the image of God led to a redefinition of the poor. "The human body in all its parts shared in the divine image," argues Ferngren.[36] This was true of everyone's body, not merely Christians' bodies. The poor, sick, and disabled were not to be shunned, but were to be seen as the objects of Christ's love. "Just as God demonstrated in the Incarnation his solidarity with those who suffer, so the members of his 'body' must demonstrate their solidarity with the suffering poor."[37] Celebration of the Eucharist allowed Christians to embrace solidarity with Christ and with all of those made in God's image. In sum, the image of God, especially as refracted through the prism of the Incarnation, formed the basis for Christian compassion and care for those in need.

Sixteenth-century Protestant theologians relied on the assumptions of earlier Christian anthropologies, even if they sometimes developed ideas in new directions. Drawing from Augustine in particular, both Luther and Calvin placed strong accent on the teaching of hereditary or Original Sin, which deformed (but did not obliterate) the creational *imago Dei* in human beings. As a consequence, it became a commonplace to view human nature as paradoxical: fallen through sin but still bearing the image of God.

35. Ibid., 102. 36. Ibid., 103.
37. Ibid.,104.

Tracing out this theme in Martin Luther's works, John Witte, Jr., has argued that a correct anthropology for the Reformers "lies in the juxtaposition of human depravity and human sanctity."[38] Luther believed that the endowments of the *imago Dei* belonged to God's human creatures from the beginning.[39] In his lectures on Genesis, for instance, Luther maintained that in the garden Adam and Eve had wills that were upright, reason that was sound, and bodies that enjoyed "the greatest dignity."[40] Just as paradise vanished after humans fell into sin, however, so the divine image retreated. "From the image of God," he said, "from the knowledge of God, from the knowledge of all other creatures, and from a very honorable nakedness man has fallen into blasphemies, into hatred, into contempt of God, yes, what is even more, into enmity against God."[41] Thus, the image of God for Luther, while not altogether forfeited, became like "a lost treasure."[42]

Luther followed this paradoxical formulation in his 1520 treatise, "The Freedom of a Christian," one of the defining texts of the Reformation. Once justified by faith, every Christian, according to Luther, is simultaneously both saint and sinner, *simul iustus et peccator*, in his famous phrase. Body/soul, flesh/spirit, sinner/saint—through the lens of this paradox we can see, wrote Luther, "the lofty dignity of the Christian."[43] Each one is equally "a lord

38. John Witte, Jr., "Between Sanctity and Depravity: Human Dignity in Protestant Perspective," in Robert P. Kraynak and Glenn Tinder, eds., *In Defense of Human Dignity: Essays for Our Time* (Notre Dame, Ind.: University of Notre Dame Press, 2003), 123.

39. Helmut Lehmann and Lewis W. Spitz, eds., *Luther's Works*, vol. 34 (Philadelphia: Muhlenberg Press, 1980), 137.

40. *Luther's Works*, 1:62–64.

41. Ibid., 1:142.

42. Ibid., 1:106.

43. Martin Luther, "The Freedom of a Christian Man," in Hans J. Hillerbrand, *The Protestant Reformation* (New York: Harper & Row, 1968), 3ff.

who is subject to no one and a priest who is subject to everyone."[44] Ultimately, the image of God will be fully restored in Christ's followers only in the eschaton, even if Christians are admonished to strive for it in the here-and-now through the process that Protestants normally call "sanctification," which flows from the free gift of God who alone justifies.[45]

John Calvin's views echoed those of Luther. In his reading of Scripture, the French Reformer thought that humanity had been created in the *imago Dei*, yet because of the fall, humanity had lost the image, or at least some of it. At times Calvin appears to be of a mixed mind on the topic, as we shall see. In his commentary on Genesis, Calvin offers the following:

Since the image of God *had been destroyed in us by the fall,* we may judge from its restoration what it originally had been. Paul says that we are transformed into the image of God by the gospel. And, according to him, spiritual regeneration is nothing else than the restoration of the same image (Colossians 3:10, and Ephesians 4:23). That he made this image to consist in righteousness and true holiness, is by the figure synecdoche; for though this is the chief part, it is not the whole of God's image. Therefore by this word the perfection of our whole nature is designated, as it appeared when Adam was endued with a right judgment, had affections in harmony with reason, had all his senses sound and well-regulated, and truly excelled in everything good. Thus the chief seat of the Divine image was in his mind and heart, where it was eminent: yet was there no part of him in which some scintillations of it did not shine forth. For there was an attempering in the several parts of the soul, which corresponded with their various offices. In the mind perfect intelligence flourished and reigned, uprightness attended as its companion, and all the senses were prepared and moulded for due obedience to reason; and in the body

44. Witte, "Between Sanctity and Depravity," 126.
45. *Luther's Works,* 1:65.

there was a suitable correspondence with this internal order. But now, although some obscure lineaments of that image are found remaining in us; yet are they so vitiated and maimed, that they may truly be said to be destroyed. For besides the deformity which everywhere appears unsightly, this evil also is added, that no part is free from the infection of sin.[46]

In the same commentary, however, offering his gloss on Genesis 9:6, Calvin seems to soften the notion that the image has been lost entirely:

For the greater confirmation of the above doctrines God declares, that he is not thus solicitous respecting human life rashly, and for no purpose. Men are indeed unworthy of God's care, if respect be had only to themselves. But *since they bear the image of God engraven on them,* He deems himself violated in their person. Thus, although they have nothing of their own by which they obtain the favor of God, he looks upon his own gifts in them, and is thereby excited to love and to care for them. This doctrine, however is to be carefully observed that no one can be injurious to his brother without wounding God himself. Were this doctrine deeply fixed in our minds, we should be much more reluctant than we are to inflict injuries. Should anyone object, that this divine image has been obliterated, the solution is easy; first, *there yet exists some remnant of it,* so that man is possessed of no small dignity; and, secondly, the Celestial Creator himself, however corrupted man may be, still keeps in view the end of his original creation; and according to his example, we ought to consider for what end he created men, and what excellence he has bestowed upon them above the rest of living beings.[47]

Finally, Calvin seemed to believe that the image was restored in human creatures through regeneration. So on Colossians 3:10, where Paul writes, "Do not lie to one another, seeing that you have put off the old self with its practices and have put on the new self,

46. John Calvin, *Calvin's Bible Commentaries, Genesis, Part I,* vol. 1, trans. John King (Edinburgh, 1846), 49 (emphasis added).
47. Ibid., 221 (emphasis added).

which is being renewed in knowledge *after the image of its creator,"*
Calvin comments:

And this is what he immediately adds, that we are renewed after the image of God. Now, the image of God resides in the whole of the soul, inasmuch as it is not the reason merely that is rectified, but also the will.
Hence, too, we learn, on the one hand, what is the end of our regeneration, that is, that we may be made like God, and that his glory may shine
forth in us; and, on the other hand, what is the image of God, of which
mention is made by Moses in Genesis 9:6, the rectitude and integrity of
the whole soul, so that man reflects, like a mirror, the wisdom, righteousness, and goodness of God. He [Paul] speaks somewhat differently in the
Epistle to the Ephesians, but the meaning is the same. See the passage—
Ephesians 4:24. Paul, at the same time, teaches that there is nothing more
excellent at which the Colossians can aspire, inasmuch as this is our
highest perfection and blessedness to bear the image of God.[48]

Interestingly (although much later and from the Methodist tradition), the twentieth-century Princeton ethicist Paul Ramsey offered a similar view of human dignity in his often-cited 1974 essay "The Indignity of 'Death with Dignity.'" In response to those
who were calling for doctors to remove life-sustaining treatment
so patients could die in "a dignified manner," Ramsey argued that
death was an inherent *in*dignity, because it "contradict[ed] ... the
unique worth of an individual human life." When human beings
were originally created, argued Ramsey, they were done so for
"perfection" in God's eternal company. Through sin came death,
so that now our dignity is what Ramsey called an "alien dignity."[49]

---

48. John Calvin, *Calvin's Bible Commentaries: Philippians, and Colossians, and Thessalonians*, vol. 42, trans. John King (Edinburgh, 1847), 180. The verse in Ephesians Calvin refers to reads: "and to clothe yourselves in the new self, created ac-
cording to the likeness of God in true righteousness and holiness" (4:24, NRSV).

49. Paul Ramsey, "The Indignity of 'Death with Dignity,'" *Hastings Center Studies* 2 (May 1974): 47–62.

In love, God offers us redemption through the crucified Christ, who provides salvation from sin and ultimately conquest of death, and, with it, the full restoration and renewal of the *imago Dei,* our highest blessedness, as Calvin had written.

ANABAPTIST AND BAPTIST

PERSPECTIVES

Early Anabaptist confessions, like the ecumenical creeds before them, contain little explicit creational anthropology. That is, the burden of these confessions seems typically to be on expounding the nature of sin and salvation (and other doctrines); they offer only limited references to what constitutes normative humanity or human nature per se. Even so, some instruction can be gleaned from them. Take, for instance, the Waterland Confession (1580), an early Anabaptist confession of the Dutch followers of Menno Simons. Its Article IV, "Of the Creation, Fall and Restitution of Man," reads as follows:

This one God created man good, according to his own image and likeness, for salvation or safety, and in him all men for the same happy end. The first man fell into sins and became subject to divine wrath, and by God was raised up again through consolatory promises and admitted to eternal life at the same time with all those who had fallen; so that none of his posterity, in respect of this restitution, is born guilty of sin or blame.[50]

Article V from the same confession, "Of the Faculty of Man Before and After the Fall," offers the following:

There was in man who was created good and was continuing in goodness, a faculty of hearing, admitting, or rejecting evil which was offered to him by the spirit of wickedness. Now in the same man, fallen and per-

50. This quote and those that follow from various Baptist confessions are from W. L. Lumpkin, *Baptist Confessions of Faith,* rev. ed. (Valley Forge, Pa.: Judson Press, 1969), 43.

verted, was a faculty of hearing, admitting or rejecting good, occurring and offered by God. For just as before the fall, hearing and admitting occurring evil, he manifested the faculty of admitting it, so also after the fall, by hearing and admitting occurring good, he shows that he has the faculty of accepting it. But that faculty of accepting or rejecting the grace of God truly offered, remains, through grace, in all his posterity.[51]

Taking the two articles together, the confession affirms that Adam was created good, made according to the image and likeness of God, was the progenitor of all humanity, and had certain natural faculties, namely, hearing, admitting, or rejecting good and evil.

A Short Confession of Faith (1610), an early English Baptist confession, practically reproduces this language in its first article using the synonymous expression, "Man being created good, and continuing in goodness, had the ability, the spirit of wickedness tempting him, freely to obey, assent, or reject the propounded evil."[52] The confession does not return to the subject of humanity again until Article XL, on resurrection and eschatology, which reads as follows:

Lastly, we believe and teach that Jesus Christ … will return from heaven with power and great glory, and with him all the holy angels, that he may be glorified in his saints and may be admired by all believers, and will manifest himself as the Judge of the living and the dead. At that time all men, just and unjust, who have lived upon the earth and have died, will rise from the dead (with incorruption) and live again, their souls being reunited with their own bodies in which they had lived evilly or well.[53]

From this article it appears that the confession teaches a type of body-soul dualism. Every individual who has lived and died will be resurrected in bodily form, albeit "with incorruption," and will be united to his or her soul, while those who are living at the

51. Ibid.,45–46.   52. Ibid.,103.
53. Ibid., 65–66.

time of Christ's return will put on "incorruption." Though it is not
stated explicitly, humanity presumably will continue to exist, either in heaven or hell, in resurrected form.

The Dordrecht Confession (1632), often regarded as the most
influential of all Mennonite confessions, contains similar language. It was drafted by Adrian Cornelis, the erstwhile bishop of
the Flemish Church in Dordrecht and signed by fifty-one ministers
from Holland and Germany. Article I, "Of God and the Creation
and All Things," begins with an affirmation of Trinitarianism, followed by a confession of God's creative activity in the world. Then
the confession takes up the creation of human beings:

> When He had finished His works and, according to His good pleasure,
> had ordained and prepared each of them, they were deemed right and
> good according to their nature, being, and quality. He created the first
> man, Adam, the father of all of us, gave him a body formed "of the dust
> of the ground, breathed into his nostrils the breath of life," so that he "be-
> came a living soul," created by God "in His own image and likeness," in
> "righteousness and true holiness" unto eternal life. He also gave him a
> place above all other creatures and endowed him with many high and ex-
> cellent gifts, put him into the garden of Eden, and gave him a command-
> ment and an interdiction.[54]

Here we have a fuller, more comprehensive treatment of the creation of Adam, his creaturely endowments, and his place in the
hierarchy of beings. There also seems to be an allusion to a creation mandate: having put Adam in the garden, God then gave
him a "commandment and an interdiction." But again, human nature *as such* is hardly mentioned throughout the remainder of the
confession, until, at the end, the confession treats the resurrection
of the dead and the last judgment in manner similar to the English Baptist *A Short Confession of Faith* (1610).

54. Ibid., 67.

Two other English confessions, crucial in shaping subsequent Baptist identity and theology, merit mentioning: the London Confession of 1644 and the Second London Confession of 1689. W. L. Lumpkin writes of the former that "no Confession of Faith has had so formative an influence on Baptist life as this one."[55] Its influence was not only felt in England, but reached into the New World as well. Having acknowledged that to be the case, however, I would argue that the confession offers nothing distinctive in its anthropology; it reiterates, "In the beginning, God made all things very good, created man after his own Image and likenesse, filling him with all perfection of all naturall excellency and uprightnesse, free from all sin."[56]

More could be said of "Old World" Baptist confessions, but if I may cross the Atlantic, so to speak, I would like to comment on several "New World" confessions and statements of faith, building up to that of the present-day Southern Baptist Convention, the largest Protestant body in the United States. Some of its creedal affirmations bear directly on discussion of human dignity today.

However, when the first Baptist churches were formed in the New World in New England and later in the Middle Colonies, as Lumpkin reminds us, they did not have their own confessions.[57] They relied on the Bible alone or used confessions produced in England. In the Southern states of Virginia and North Carolina, the earliest Baptists were heavily Arminian and affirmed the Standard General Baptist Confession, which had been presented to King Charles II of England on July 26, 1660.

The Philadelphia Association of Baptists, founded in 1707, bears the distinction of being the first Baptist association on American

---

55. Ibid., 52. It is based, however, on the still older so-called True Confession of 1596.

56. Ibid., 157.

57. Ibid., 347.

soil. According to Lumpkin, "The earliest known reference by an association to a confession occurred in 1724, when the Philadelphia Association, referred to 'the Confession of Faith, set forth by the elders and brethren met in London, 1689, and owned by us.'"[58] What was officially adopted in 1742 as the Philadelphia Confession was identical to the Second London Confession (1689), with the exception of Articles XXIII and XXXI, on singing songs other than the Psalms, and on the imposition of hands on baptized believers, respectively.

Following the Great Awakening in New England, Separate Baptists arose who distinguished themselves from their Congregational forebears because of their insistence on "experimental religion." While they generally disfavored confessions, they did agree to adopt a so-called Ten Principles of Faith. Of those principles, two are concerned with anthropology. Article III treats the subject of human sinfulness, mentioning that "Adam fell from his original state of purity." There is no reference to the image of God, to the creation mandate, or to human faculties. In Article V, the confession affirms "that there will be a resurrection from the dead, and a general or universal judgment, and that the happiness of the righteous and punishment of the wicked will be eternal."[59] The confessional minimalism typical of Baptists excluded other possible affirmations about human nature, but we could assume they affirmed much else, though drawing directly from the pages of Scripture.

As the Free Will Baptist movement gained influence after 1780, Baptists in New Hampshire sought to moderate some of the Calvinism they had inherited from their British Particular Baptist brethren. Accordingly, on June 24, 1830, the Baptists of New

58. Ibid., 349.
59. Ibid., 358.

Hampshire appointed a committee to draft a new declaration of faith and practice. One of those commissioned to review the draft was John Newton Brown, who, twenty years later, as editorial secretary of the American Baptist Publication Society, would include the confession in his widely circulated *The Baptist Church Manual*, thus insuring it great influence for all subsequent Baptists.

Like some of the confessions before it, the New Hampshire Confession had little to say directly about human nature as created by God. In fact, there is no mention of the image of God or created human faculties. Article III, "Of the Fall of Man," declares: "[We believe] that man was created in a state of holiness, under the law of his Maker; but by voluntary transgression fell from that holy and happy state."[60] A later article on the nature of humanity following bodily death and the resurrection is equally vague: "[We believe] that the end of this world is approaching: that at the last day, Christ will descend from heaven, and raise the dead from the grave to final retribution; that a solemn separation will then take place; that the wicked will be adjudged to endless punishment, and the righteous to endless joy."[61] Beyond these affirmations, there is little explicit instruction contained in the confession about the nature of our humanity.

Present-day Southern Baptists came into their own only in the twentieth century, even if they are the legatees of older Baptist movements. Drawing from the New Hampshire Confession of Faith, the Southern Baptist Convention produced the Baptist Faith and Message in 1925, revised in 1963 and, more recently, in 2000. The first version was adopted the same year as the famous Scopes trial in Dayton, Tennessee, and we might conclude that Baptists felt pressed at this time to reflect more intentionally upon

60. Ibid., 362.
61. Ibid., 367.

created human nature. Reflecting the controversy over evolution during that era, the *Southern Baptist Convention Annual* of 1924 shows that an unsuccessful effort was made by C. P. Stealey of Oklahoma to modify Article III to read: "We believe man came into the world by direct creation of God, and not by evolution. This creative act was separate and distinct from any other work of God and was not conditioned upon antecedent changes in previously created forms of life." The actual 1925 (and later 1963) version of the Baptist Faith and Message, however, affirmed the following under Article III, "Man":

Man was created by the special act of God, in His own image, and is the crowning work of His creation. In the beginning man was innocent of sin and was endowed by his Creator with freedom of choice. By his free choice man sinned against God and brought sin into the human race. Through the temptation of Satan man transgressed the command of God, and fell from his original innocence; whereby his posterity inherit a nature and an environment inclined toward sin, and as soon as they are capable of moral action become transgressors and are under condemnation. Only the grace of God can bring man into His holy fellowship and enable man to fulfill creative purpose of God. The sacredness of human personality is evident in that God created man in His own image, and in that Christ died for man; therefore every man possesses dignity and is worthy of respect and Christian love.[62]

While no mention of "evolution" appeared in the 1925 version of the Baptist Faith and Message, this article nevertheless affirms the "special creation" of man. Furthermore, going farther than past confessions, the article states that man is made in the image of God and has a unique place in the created order as "the crowning work" of God's creation. While much of the remainder of the

62. 1925 Statement of Baptist Faith and Message, accessed at http://www.reformedreader.org/ccc/1925bfam.htm (February 2, 2011).

article addresses the problem of human sinfulness, the conclusion speaks of the "sacredness of human personality," a result of God's having created humanity in his own image. Presumably, this sacredness is further expounded in the expression "therefore every man possesses *dignity* and is worthy of respect and Christian love."[63] To my knowledge, this is the first usage of the word dignity in an American, Baptist creedal statement.

A significant revision of the Baptist Faith & Message was adopted by the Southern Baptist Convention at its annual meeting in June 2000. Several features of Article III ("Man") stand out and provide a richer anthropology than past documents, while some of its other articles connect its teaching on anthropology to a social ethic. Article III reads as follows:

Man is the special creation of God, made in His own image. He created them male and female as the crowning work of His creation. The gift of gender is thus part of the goodness of God's creation. In the beginning man was innocent of sin and was endowed by his Creator with freedom of choice. By his free choice man sinned against God and brought sin into the human race. Through the temptation of Satan man transgressed the command of God, and fell from his original innocence whereby his posterity inherit a nature and an environment inclined toward sin. Therefore, as soon as they are capable of moral action, they become transgressors and are under condemnation. Only the grace of God can bring man into His holy fellowship and enable man to fulfill the creative purpose of God. The sacredness of human personality is evident in that God created man in His own image, and in that Christ died for man; therefore, every person of every race possesses full dignity and is worthy of respect and Christian love.[64]

63. Ibid. (emphasis added).

64. 2000 Statement of Baptist Faith and Message, accessed at http://www.sbc .net/bfm/bfm2000.asp (February 2, 2011).

As in some earlier creeds, the article affirms that gender was part of God's original design—"He created them male and female"—and that gender is one of God's good gifts to humanity. Moreover, as with the original statement, the Baptist Faith and Message of 2000 insists on the sanctity of the human person: "Every person of every race possesses full dignity." Given the sad, long shadow of slavery and segregation in American history in general and Southern Baptist history in particular, the article is at pains to stress racial unity and "full" dignity.

Articles XV and XVIII of the Baptist Faith and Message 2000 also merit brief mention. The former, "On the Christian and the Social Order," indicates that "we should speak on behalf of the unborn and contend for the sanctity of all human life from conception to natural death." Here, the emphasis is not on the "sanctity of the personality," as in the earlier article, but on the "sanctity of human life."[65] Doubtlessly, the phrase "from conception to natural death" means to signify the period of human physical embodiment. The sanctity of human life is a doctrine that is firmly established in the more recent history of the Southern Baptist Convention.[66] Finally, Article XVIII, "The Family," affirms that "husband and wife are of equal worth before God, since both are created in God's image." Here the *imago Dei* is explicitly invoked as the ground of equality between spouses, and presumably between genders more generally.

65. It might have been preferable to use the word "every" instead of "all" to modify "human life." As it reads, the statement could imply the sanctity of life *qua* life. "Every human life" would imply, as I think the authors of the Baptist Faith and Message 2000 meant to say, that they make no distinction between human *lives* and human *persons*. Every human being is a human person.

66. For a discussion of the history of Southern Baptist resolutions on the sanctity of human life, see C. Ben Mitchell, "Southern Baptists and Bioethics," in John F. Peppin, Mark J. Cherry, and Ana Iltis, eds., *Annals of Bioethics: Religious Perspectives in Bioethics* (New York: Taylor & Francis, 2004), 97–108.

CONCLUSION

What lessons can we learn from this *tour d'horizon* of scriptural sources, Reformers' commentary, and Anabaptist and Baptist confessional statements? For starters, we might note that a creational anthropology has received less attention than one might expect—especially if one compares it to teachings on the Incarnation, Trinity, Fall, etc. This is perhaps understandable in light of the fact that only relatively recently has the church come face to face with truly revolutionary questions about the very meaning of humanity—questions arising especially from the fields of biology, psychology, and neuroscience. Historically and often reflecting intra-Protestant polemics, most of the attention given to anthropology has centered on the effects of sin and the work of the Holy Spirit in regeneration and sanctification. Controversy about human nature per se was muted prior to the twentieth century. Arguably, our present century poses yet more complex challenges and will require the best Christian minds to devote greater attention to understanding our humanity in theological, philosophical, and scientific terms.

But Baptists, along with other Christians, are also connected to the broader intellectual patrimony of the West, which is suffused with the idea of human dignity (and human rights derived therefrom). From the Magna Carta (1215), to the French Declaration of the Rights of Man and Citizen (1789), to the U.S. Bill of Rights (1791), the assumption of human worth, reflecting traces of the ancient biblical teaching of *imago Dei,* has nourished the affirmation of the solidarity, rights, and obligations of human beings living in community.

As others in this volume have noted, the idea of human dignity faces complex challenges today. To offer one example, the philosopher of animal rights Peter Singer vilifies anyone who harps on human dignity by labeling him or her a "speciesist," someone who should be held in at least as much contempt as a racist or chauvinist. What is more, as Thomas Albert Howard and Father John Behr have noted in this book, Harvard's Steven Pinker has called the idea of human dignity a patent "stupidity" and an "almost useless concept."

Recent agnosticism about human dignity has led to suspicion of the very idea of "inalienable" human rights. Those who have been influenced by the social constructivism of the mainstream academy tend to see rights as a mere construct, a useful myth, little more than a necessary capitulation to prevent anarchy.[67] Following the late philosopher Richard Rorty, many believe that we can subscribe to a belief in human rights only in a spirit of "irony."[68]

Are we finally left with human rights as myth, still affirmed, albeit ironically? Is the Western foundation for human personhood an apparition? If so, we are perhaps of all generations to be most pitied. Perhaps, though, the Judeo-Christian anthropology, with its acknowledgment of the special dignity of human beings, can again help underwrite a coherent conception of human rights. While Christians have not always lived up to the moral demands of their anthropology, it has undeniably, both explicitly and implicitly, helped fuel many major moral developments in history, including the repudiation of infanticide, abortion, and euthanasia; the abolition of slavery and the slave trade; the social equality and suffrage of women; the revulsion toward Nazi war crimes and other twentieth-century genocides. And it has nourished our intuitions that torture, child abuse, and exploitation of human beings are not simply distasteful, but morally repugnant.

67. For a trenchant, nuanced analysis of social constructivism as it bears on language of human rights, see Thomas L. Haskell, "The Curious Persistence of Rights Talk in the 'Age of Interpretation,'" *Journal of American History* 74 (December 1987): 984–1012.

68. Richard Rorty, *Contingency, Irony, and Solidarity* (New York: Cambridge University Press, 1989).

Let me conclude then with a plea that the ideas of human dignity and human rights in the West would benefit from a reconnection to their taproot: the conception of the human person offered in biblical religion and in its many creedal manifestations throughout the ages, including those of my own Protestant-Baptist tradition. Put differently, a firm foundation for natural or inalienable human rights, predicated on a belief in human dignity, is found in biblical religion in a special way. The Princeton professor of ethics Max Stackhouse puts it this way:

Certainly we cannot say that all of Judaism or of Christianity has supported human rights. It has been key minorities within these traditions, arguing their case over long periods of time, that have established the normative view. Nor can we say that even these groups have been faithful to the implications of their own heritage at all times, and the horror stories of our pasts also have to be told to mitigate any temptation to triumphalism. Still, intellectual honesty demands recognition of the fact that what passes as "secular," "Western" principles of basic human rights developed nowhere else but out of key strands of biblically rooted religions.[69]

Human rights, in other words, are not ahistorical, free-floating principles that can be untethered from their religious and moral origins without potential peril. The word "dignity" comes from the Latin *dignitas* ("worth") and *dignus* ("worthy"). When applied to Homo sapiens, the etymology suggests that human beings should be understood as having inherent value and each member of the species should be treated with special respect. Over against the stratification of an Aristotelian caste system or the ironic incredulity of contemporary sophisticates, the Western genesis of human dignity presumes an abiding value vested in human beings by a loving Creator.

69. Max L. Stackhouse, "Why Human Rights Needs God: A Christian Perspective," in Elizabeth M. Bucar and Barbara Barnett, eds., *Does Human Rights Need God?* (Grand Rapids, Mich.: William B. Eerdmans, 2005), 33.

As we have seen, various strands of theology and creedal statements, echoing Scripture, anchor human worth or worthiness in the fact that we were made in the "image and likeness" of our Creator (Gn 1:27); and thus all human beings, irrespective of differences, bear that image.

For Christians, of course, the truest amplitude of human worth is revealed in the Incarnation—the enfleshment—of God in the person of Jesus of Nazareth. Through the Incarnation God sacralized humanity in Christ's "taking the very nature of a servant, being made in human likeness" (Phil 2:7). Consequently, Christians find the dignity of the human person made most manifest in the face of Jesus. The councils of the early Christian church spent much time and energy working out what it means theologically for God to become a human person. While the Protestant Reformers took what we have called a "paradoxical" view of the *imago Dei,* they, too, nevertheless saw the image of God in the face of Jesus Christ and those who shared his corporeal nature.

The notion of human dignity has been foundational to modern civilization, not least through its doctrinal entailments of freedom of conscience, freedom of speech, and freedom of religion. John Witte, Jr., may be right when he says that "today, the concept of human dignity has become ubiquitous to the point of cliché—a moral trump frayed by heavy use, a general principle harried by constant invocation."[70] But the way forward, in my view, is not to cease invoking the idea, but to rehabilitate its meaning and use, by making clear its intellectual and specifically theological foundations. In our biotechnological age, the consequences of forfeiting the creational ground of respect for every individual human life—and for the human community as a whole—seem too grotesque to contemplate, but too likely to ignore.

70. Witte, "Between Sanctity and Depravity," 121.

AFTERWORD

GILBERT C. MEILAENDER

THE three essays gathered here constitute an ecumenical conversation about important ideas that merit our attention. One speaker in the conversation draws on the Fathers of the Christian church (and especially, some of the Eastern Fathers); another draws primarily on the high scholastic thought of St. Thomas and on authoritative papal teaching of the last two centuries; a third draws primarily on the scriptures of the Old and New Testaments as well as Protestant confessional statements. Yet, they enter the conversation not only as representatives of different Christian traditions and communions but also as those who have one Lord, and share one faith, and (if we are to take St. Paul seriously) are members of one body.

Conversations, of course, are often open-ended affairs. Whatever issue triggers a conversation, it is likely to wander here and there, leaving us hard pressed to specify with any precision a single subject that is its point. More-over, it can be just as hard to say when—or if—a conversation has ended. We can always reopen it and continue at a later time, in-tervening at one point or another in search of greater clarity or to sharpen points of agreement or disagreement.

In this afterword I think of myself as continuing the conver-sation, even though I enter it only via words on a printed page and not *viva voce*. Coming late in this way to the conversation, the first question we might ask—and it's not, I think, a simple one to answer in the case of this conversation—is, just what is it *about?* The editor of this volume gives us, actually, several possibilities, though whether the essays connect all the dots is harder to say. Perhaps the conversation's point is to ask, "How might Christians today think well and wisely about human dignity?" Perhaps the point—is it a different or the same point?—is to explore how the notion of the "image of God" helps to illumine and clarify our understanding of human dignity. Or, to notice a different feature of this particular conversation, the point may be to see whether those who speak out of specifically different strands of the Chris-tian tradition can talk together—and, perhaps, enrich each oth-er's understanding—of a concept that is shared by their different strands. Or, yet one more possibility, the conversation may be in-tended to probe a related but somewhat different question: wheth-er there is any helpful way to bring the specifically theological language of these branches of Christian thought to bear on con-troverted public questions in a society such as ours.

In fact, the conversation gathered together and written down in these pages is about all of these things, and I will try to say a brief word about each of them. This cannot, of course, be a defini-tive word, as if anyone could unilaterally declare a conversation finished. It is nothing more, really, than an attempt to think along with our three interlocutors—Behr, Hittinger, Mitchell—but in a way that raises further questions, voices concerns and hesitations, and, hence, continues the conversation.

Although one aim of the conversation was to ask how Christian language about the *imago Dei* might help us understand human dignity, I would have to say that our three conversation partners—Mitchell, perhaps, excepted—explore *imago* more than *dignitas*. Whether this really helps us with the serious questions about human dignity that we face in our society is not entirely clear to me. If "dignity" is a puzzling concept, signifying several different things, the "image of God" is at least as confusing. Despite its importance in the history of Christian thought, actual biblical uses of it are rather sparse, leaving open several different ways of unpacking its meaning.

Ben Mitchell calls our attention to—and largely, I think, endorses—a "functional" understanding of the *imago*. It depends on characterizing humankind not as created "in" the image of God but created "as" the image of God—to function, that is, as God's representative by governing, tending, and caring for the rest of the creation. Simply as a way of understanding the biblical concept, this is an attractive suggestion, but, if we take this approach, it becomes even harder to know how, if at all, it might shed light on that other concept, human dignity. Moreover, it may seem to some that man is well suited to function "as" God's representative because he is made "in" God's image—and, hence, that some understanding of the latter idea is still needed to ground the former.

The two standard—to some degree complementary, to some degree competing—understandings of humankind as made "in" the image of God are often characterized as "substantive" and "relational," as Mitchell notes. The substantive understanding points to some feature of human nature—for example, rationality—that sets humankind apart from the rest of the animal creation. The relational understanding thinks of human beings as in God's image when they live in right relationship to God, entering into the giving and receiving of love that characterizes the divine life. These two understandings can, then, be conjoined if we think of the relational as an image that can be lost through sin and the substantive as capable of persisting (though, no doubt, darkened or distorted) even in our sin. How or whether these notions help us understand human dignity is a question to which I will return shortly.

Both John Behr and Russell Hittinger complicate these somewhat standard approaches, however. Behr does so by connecting the "image" less with human *nature* than with human *destiny* (that is, our eschatological destiny to be conformed to the nature of Christ). He is prepared, therefore, to say that "we have yet to become human." I suspect that readers might both understand what he means by this and yet find it puzzling. We are, after all, talking about human beings, not dogs. We must therefore be able to identify them, even if that identification is in some sense provisional. In other words, we must be able to talk not only about destiny but also about nature.

But, in any case, if we do focus on the *imago* as our destiny in Christ, how would this connect to the idea of human dignity? To be honest, I'm not sure, but I think Behr could say that it would lead us to see in every human being a possible (though by no means guaranteed) future companion in beatitude. This helps, no doubt, to explain why Behr suggests that "human being" is a more fundamental category than "person." It helps, but it does not persuade me—at least not if we're looking for some sort of payoff in increased understanding of dignity. For part of what has made dignity an important, and controversial, topic is that it suggests that each person is marked individually by the God-relation and is not simply a member of a species prone to extinction. About each person there is what John Crosby has called an "unrepeat-ability." This unrepeatability brings with it incommensurability, makes judgments of comparative dignity impossible, and affirms the fundamental equality of human persons.[1]

Russell Hittinger complicates standard understandings in a different manner. Making his way through a complex but fasci-nating several centuries of development in Roman Catholic social thought, he argues that the *imago Dei* may be seen not just in in-dividual human beings but also in some forms of human commu-nity (such as marriage in the order of creation and the church in the order of redemption). As a way of overcoming or transcend-ing some dangers of an emphasis on isolated "individuals," this is an important line of inquiry. (It's not entirely new, however. What Roman Catholic magisterial thought achieved slowly and labori-ously in its complex development within a tradition, Karl Barth achieved in a somewhat more intuitive burst of theological in-sight—locating the *imago* precisely in the mutual giving and re-ceiving of marriage that images the giving and receiving within the divine life.)[2] If, though, we are looking for help in understand-ing human dignity, I'm not sure that avoiding unwarranted indi-vidualism is to the point. Hittinger sees this, to be sure, noting that one cannot expunge from the tradition the "moment of soli-tude" that invests each person with the image of God. Thus, in his own way he points to the unrepeatability of each person, which makes possible the equal dignity of human persons.

Were I to have had the opportunity to enter more directly into this conversation, and not join it only after the fact, I think I would have wanted to ask all three speakers whether they were sure that explicating the "image of God" was the best—or, even,

1. John F. Crosby, "The Twofold Source of the Dignity of Persons," *Faith and Philosophy* 18 (July 2001): 292–306.

2. Karl Barth, *Church Dogmatics, III/1* (Edinburgh: T. & T. Clark, 1958), 184–206.

a helpful—way of working through the various puzzles raised by controversies in our culture about human dignity. The sheer complexity of these puzzles gives rise to caution on my part—though, to be sure, we cannot assume the conversation is over.

Whatever our conclusion on that score, the other large issue raised by the conversation has to do with something quite intentional in its structure. The three speakers represent distinctively different ecclesial traditions within Christianity, and were, the editor tells us, specifically asked to speak out of their respective ecclesial standpoints.

Did it work? Do we have the sense that all three are really talking about, roughly, the same thing? Or, as is so often the case in our own conversations, have the interlocutors sometimes passed each other by? Obviously, in some senses they are talking about the same thing: each knows of that (sparse) set of scriptural passages that refer to the *imago Dei*. Yet, they move in quite different directions. Mitchell is principally concerned with how the concept of the image of God can ground a Christian anthropology in our created nature. Behr is more focused on our destiny than our nature. And Hittinger aims especially to eliminate any improperly individualistic tendencies from our understanding of human nature. Family resemblances crop up here and there throughout the conversation—and a good thing for the "one body" that they do—but, nevertheless, they are playing quite different instruments in the orchestra, and it's not evident how much assistance any one of them can be to the others in sorting through their own distinctive worries. I'm not certain, therefore, how fruitful for ecumenical convergence the topic of the *imago Dei* is. We might do better to interpret their efforts as enriching and expanding—and, perhaps, complicating—the ecumenical imperative extolled by the editor.

Suppose, though, we bracket this issue and focus instead on a related concern of the conference in which the conversation began: namely, whether these several forms of distinctively Christian language can be helpful in *public* discussion of controversies surrounding human dignity. Behr seems to have his doubts, as well he might given the understanding of the *imago* that he has defended. "However it is we define what constitutes the existence of human beings as created in the image of God," he writes, "we are still confronted with the anomaly that this truth is not at all self-evident."

I myself find this a questionable way to frame the problem. How many views set forth in public argument are self-evident? Were self-evidence the standard, public debate would be a pretty quiet affair. The problem is better described in a way Hittinger explores: can we make public appeals to things we (think we) know not on the basis of reason but only on the basis of special revelation? Hittinger is doubtful and prefers to look for ways in which common human experience and reasoned reflection may discern in human life intimations of truths more fully revealed in the revelation of our creation in God's image.

Perhaps we should allow ourselves to wonder, though, whether viewpoints, claims, and arguments that go beyond common human experience or widely shared reasons might not have an important place in public discussion. We owe each other, our fellow citizens, an honest articulation of the considerations that move us to think as we do. Suppose John Behr tells me, his fellow citizen, that he thinks every human being is possessed of an inviolable dignity, and I ask him why in the world he thinks that. He should tell me that he, like other Christians, believes that our human life has been taken up into the life of the risen Christ and renewed in such a way that every human being we meet is a possible future companion in beatitude. I may not believe that. I may even think it bizarre. But there is nothing rationally inaccessible about it. Understanding it, I understand a little better why he thinks as he does. And, I suspect, even if I do not share his view, I may nonetheless find it rather moving and deserving of respect in our shared civic life.

I don't suppose, of course, that it would be terribly useful for Russell Hittinger to carry into public debate the complex account he has given of the twists and turns in the development of Roman Catholic social teaching on the *imago Dei*. But it might be useful for him to help us understand that he and his fellow believers think that the created human nature we share will be perfected and completed in Christ; that, moreover, this means that each of us always exists as an individual-in-relation (a truth imaged even in certain bonds of ordinary human life); and that, therefore, however great or few our individual capacities may be, it is the task given each of us to draw one another into shared bonds of love.

To be honest, though, I suspect that it is Mitchell's specifically biblical language that may have the greatest public purchase. Dependent less on a developed theological or philosophical system, it makes contact at a level that is deeper still, the level of a story in whose plot both human nature and human destiny play central roles. This language is common Christian language, though of course (as the conversation put in print here demonstrates) it will be taken in somewhat different directions and given different nuance by those who speak out of different strands of the Christian tradition. And as common Christian language it has not lost its power—even in our late-modern world. I say this, of course, as one who is, like Mitchell, a Protestant (though of a rather different sort). But that is only to say that this important conversation has not ended and that it has many twists and turns that I have not explored here.

SELECTED
BIBLIOGRAPHY

Amesbury, Richard. *Faith and Human Rights: Christianity and the Global Struggle for Human Dignity.* Minneapolis: Fortress Press, 2008.

Archer, Margaret S. *Being Human: The Problem of Agency.* Cambridge: Cambridge University Press, 2000.

Archer, Margaret S., and Pierpaolo Donati, eds. *Pursuing the Common Good.* Pontifical Academy of Social Sciences, *Acta* 14 (Vatican City, 2008), 75–123.

Atkin, Bill, and Katrine Evans. *Human Rights and the Common Good, Christian Perspectives.* Wellington: Victoria University Press, 1999.

Baillie, Harold W., and Timothy E. Casey, eds. *Is Human Nature Obsolete? Genetics, Bioengineering, and the Future of the Human Condition.* Cambridge, Mass.: MIT Press, 2005.

Bloch, Ernst. *Natural Law and Human Dignity.* Translated by Dennis J. Schmidt. Cambridge, Mass.: MIT Press, 1996.

Bloom, Irene, J. Paul Martin, and Wayne Proudfoot. *Religious Diversity and Human Rights.* New York: Columbia University Press, 1996.

Brown, Warren S., Nancey Murphy, and H. Newton Malony, eds. *Whatever Happened to the Soul? Scientific and Theological Portraits of Human Nature.* Minneapolis: Fortress Press, 1998.

Bucar, Elizabeth M., and Barbara Barnett, eds. *Does Human Rights Need God?* Grand Rapids, Mich.: Eerdmans, 2005.

Clines, D. J. A. "The Image of God in Man." *Tyndale Bulletin* 19 (1968): 53–103.

Collins, Francis S., and Victor A. McKusick. "Implications of the Human Genome Project for Medical Science." *Journal of the American Medical Association* 285 (February 7, 2001): 540–44.

Colson, Charles W., and Nigel M. de S. Cameron, eds. *Human Dignity in the Biotech Century.* Downers Grove, Ill.: InterVarsity Press, 2004.

Crosby, John F. "The Twofold Source of Human Dignity." *Faith and Philosophy* 18 (July 2001): 292–306.

de Koninck, Charles. "The Primacy of the Common Good against the Personalists." In *The Writings of Charles De Koninck,* translated by Ralph McInerny, vol. 2. Notre Dame, Ind.: University of Notre Dame Press, 2009.

Edgar, Brian. "Biotheology: Theology, Ethics and the New Biotechnologies." *Evangelical Review of Theology* 30 (July 2006): 219–36.

Elbach, Ulrich. "Protection of Life and Human Dignity: The German Debate Between Christian Norms and Secular Expectations." *Christian Bioethics: Non-Ecumenical Studies in Medical Morality* 14 (April 2008): 58–77.

Elshtain, Jean Bethke. "The Dignity of the Human Person and the Idea of Human Rights: Four Inquiries." *Journal of Law and Religion* 14 (1999–2000): 53–65.

———. *Who Are We? Critical Reflections and Hopeful Possibilities.* Grand Rapids, Mich.: Eerdmans, 2000.

Feenstra, R. J., and C. Plantinga, Jr., eds. *Trinity, Incarnation and Atonement.* Notre Dame, Ind.: University of Notre Dame Press, 1989.

Ferngren, Gary B. *Medicine and Health Care in Early Christianity.* Baltimore: Johns Hopkins University Press, 2009.

Fukuyama, Francis. *Our Posthuman Future: Consequences of the Biotechnology Revolution.* New York: Farrar, Straus & Giroux, 2002.

Grand, Steve. *Creation: Life and How to Make It.* Cambridge, Mass.: Harvard University Press, 2001.

Guttmacher, A. E., and F. S. Collins. "Genomic Medicine: A Primer." *New England Journal of Medicine* 347 (November 7, 2002): 1512–20.

Hart, David Bentley. *Atheist Delusions: The Christian Revolution and Its Fashionable Enemies.* New Haven, Conn.: Yale University Press, 2009.

Iglesias, Teresa. "Bedrock Truths and the Dignity of the Individual." *Logos* 4 (2001): 114–34.

Jewett, Paul K., and Marguerite Shuster. *Who We Are: Our Dignity as Human.* Grand Rapids, Mich.: Eerdmans, 1996.

John Paul II. *Man and Woman He Created Them: A Theology of the Body.* Translated by Michael Waldstein. Boston: Pauline Books, 2006.

Kass, Leon. *Life, Liberty, and the Defense of Dignity.* San Francisco: Encounter Books, 2002.

————. "Defending Human Dignity." *Commentary* 124 (December 2007): 53–61.

Kavanaugh, John F. *Who Count as Persons? Human Identity and the Ethics of Killing.* Washington, D.C.: Georgetown University Press, 2001.

Kilby, Karen. "Perichoresis and Projection: Problems with Social Doctrines of the Trinity." *New Blackfriars* 81 (2000): 432–45.

Kilner, John F., Arlene B. Miller, and Edmund D. Pellegrino, eds. *Dignity and Dying, A Christian Appraisal.* Grand Rapids, Mich.: Eerdmans, 1996.

————, Rebecca D. Pentz, and Frank E. Young, eds. *Genetic Ethics, Do the Ends Justify the Means?* Grand Rapids, Mich.: Eerdmans, 1997.

Kraynak, Robert P., and Glenn Tinder, eds. *In Defense of Human Dignity: Essays for Our Time.* Notre Dame, Ind.: University of Notre Dame Press, 2003.

Kurzweil, Ray. *The Singularity Is Near: When Humans Transcend Biology.* New York: Viking, 2005.

Lossky, V. *In the Image and Likeness of God.* Crestwood N.Y.: St. Vladimir's Seminary Press, 2001.

MacIntyre, Alasdair C. *After Virtue: A Study of Moral Theory,* 2nd edition. London: Duckworth, 1985.

Macklin, Ruth. "Dignity Is a Useless Concept." *British Medical Journal* 327 (December 20–27, 2003): 1419–20.

Manent, Pierre. *The City of Man.* Translated by Marc A. LePain. Princeton, N.J.: Princeton University Press, 1998.

Maritain, Jacques. Introduction to *UNESCO, Human Rights: Comments and Interpretations.* London: Wingate, 1949.

————. *Man and the State.* Chicago: University of Chicago Press, 1951.

Meilaender, Gilbert. *Neither Beast nor God: The Dignity of the Human Person.* New York: Encounter Books, 2009.

Menzel, Peter, and Faith D'Aluisio. *Robo sapiens: Evolution of a New Species.* Cambridge, Mass.: MIT Press, 2000.

Middleton, J. Richard. *The Liberating Image: The "Imago Dei" in Genesis 1.* Grand Rapids, Mich.: Brazos Press, 2005.

Murray, Paul D., ed. *Receptive Ecumenism and the Call to Catholic Learning: Exploring a Way for Contemporary Ecumenism.* New York: Oxford University Press, 2008.

Oden, Thomas. *The Rebirth of Orthodoxy: New Signs of Life in Christianity.* San Francisco: HarperSanFrancisco, 2003.

Pawlikowski, John T. "Creating an Ethical Context for Globalization: Catholic Perspectives in an Interreligious Context." *Journal of Ecumenical Studies* 42 (Summer 2007): 363–72.

Peppin, John F., Mark J. Cherry, and Ana Iltis, eds. *Annals of Bioethics: Religious Perspectives in Bioethics.* New York: Taylor & Francis, 2004.

Pinker, Steven. "The Stupidity of Dignity." *The New Republic,* May 28, 2008, 28–31.

President's Council on Bioethics. *Human Dignity and Bioethics: Essays Commissioned by the President's Council on Bioethics.* Washington, D.C., 2008.

Putnam, Hilary. *Reason, Truth, and History.* Cambridge: Cambridge University Press, 1982.

Rae, Scott, and Paul M. Cox. *Bioethics, A Christian Approach in a Pluralistic Age.* Grand Rapids, Mich.: Eerdmans, 1999.

Rahner, K. *The Trinity.* Translated by J. Donceel. Tunbridge Wells: Burns & Oates, 1986.

Ramsey, Paul. "The Indignity of 'Death with Dignity.'" *Hastings Center Studies* 2 (May 1974): 47–62.

Regan, Ethna. *Theology and the Boundary Discourse of Human Rights.* Washington D.C.: Georgetown University Press, 2010.

Rudman, Stanley. *Concepts of Persons and Christian Ethics.* Cambridge: Cambridge University Press, 1997.

Ryder, Richard. "All Beings that Feel Pain Deserve Human Rights." *The Guardian,* August 6, 2005, 20.

Sandel, Michael. *The Case Against Perfection: Ethics in the Age of Genetic Engineering.* Cambridge, Mass.: Harvard University Press, 2007.

Shepherd, Frederick M., ed. *Christianity and Human Rights: Christians and the Struggle for Global Justice.* Lanham, Md.: Lexington Books, 2009.

Sherlock, Charles. *The Doctrine of Humanity.* Downers Grove, Ill.: InterVarsity Press, 1996.

Smith, Christian. *What Is a Person?: Rethinking Humanity, Social Life, and the Moral Good From the Person Up.* Chicago: University of Chicago Press, 2010.

Sutton, Agneta. *Christian Bioethics: A Guide for the Perplexed.* New York: T&T Clark, 2008.

Taylor, Charles. *Sources of the Self.* Cambridge, Mass.: Harvard University Press, 1989.

Tertullian. *On the Resurrection of the Flesh,* 6th ed. Translated by E. Evans. London: SPCK, 1960.

Trayer, Robert. *Faith in Human Rights: Support in Religious Traditions for a Global Struggle.* Washington D.C.: Georgetown University Press, 1991.

Vorster, Nico. "The Value of Human Life." *Ecumenical Review* 59 (April–July 2007): 363–83.

White, John, and Frank S. Alexander. *Christianity and Human Rights: An Introduction.* New York: Cambridge University Press, 2010.

Witte, John, and Frank Alexander, eds. *The Teachings of Modern Roman Catholicism: On Law, Politics, and Human Nature.* 2 vols. New York: Columbia University Press, 2007.

Witte, John, and Johan D. van der Vyver. *Religious Human Rights in Global Perspective.* The Hague: Martinus Nijhoff, 1996.

Wright, Robert. *The Moral Animal: The New Science of Evolutionary Psychology.* New York: Vintage, 1995.

CONTRIBUTORS

THOMAS ALBERT (TAL) HOWARD is professor of history and director of the Center for Faith and Inquiry at Gordon College in Wenham, Massachusetts. He holds a Ph.D. in European intellectual history from the University of Virginia and is the is author of *God and the Atlantic: America, Europe and the Religious Divide; Protestant Theology and the Making of the Modern German University;* and *Religion and the Rise of Historicism,* and he is the editor of *The Future of Christian Learning: An Evangelical and Catholic Dialogue* by Mark Noll and James Turner.

FR. JOHN BEHR is dean and professor of patristics at St. Vladimir's Orthodox Theological Seminary and a distinguished lecturer in Patristics at Fordham University. He is the author or editor of numerous books, including *Irenaeus of Lyons: Identifying Christianity; The Case against Diodore and Theodore; Asceticism and Anthropology in Irenaeus and Clement; St Athanasius: On the Incarnation,* translation and introduction, Popular Patristics Series; *The Mystery of Christ: Life in Death;* and *Abba: The Tradition of Orthodoxy in the West.*

F. RUSSELL HITTINGER is the William K. Warren Professor of Catholic Studies, Department of Philosophy and Religion, and research professor of law, University of Tulsa. He is an internationally recognized contributor to contemporary debates in jurisprudence, law, and ethics and has held professorships at the Catholic University of America, Princeton University, Fordham University, and New York University. He is a member of the Pontifical Academy of St. Thomas Aquinas and the Pontifical Academy of Social Sciences. His many publications include *Thomas Aquinas and the Rule of Law;*

The First Grace: Rediscovering Natural Law in a Post-Christian Age; A Critique of the New Natural Law Theory; and *Paper Wars: The Papacy and the Modern State* (forthcoming).

C. BEN MITCHELL is Graves Professor of Moral Philosophy at Union University, where he is senior co-editor of *Renewing Minds: A Journal of Christian Thought.* He has served as co-director for Biotechnology Policy and Fellow of the Council for Biotechnology Policy in Washington, D.C., as well as a fellow of the Institute for Biotechnology and a Human Future at Illinois Institute of Technology, Chicago-Kent School of Law. He is a widely published author and was a member of the Templeton Oxford Summer Symposium on Religion and Science, 2003–2005. He is editor of the journal *Ethics & Medicine: An International Journal of Bioethics.* He is the author of *Ethics and Moral Reasoning,* a contributor to *Faith and Learning: A Handbook for Christian Higher Education,* edited by David S. Dockery, and co-author of *Biotechnology and the Human Good.*

GILBERT C. MEILAENDER holds the Richard and Phyllis Duesenberg Chair in Theological Ethics at Valparaiso University. In 2002, he was appointed a member of the President's Council on Bioethics. He is associate editor for the *Journal of Religious Ethics* and a fellow of the Hastings Center. His many books include *Neither Beast Nor God: The Dignity of the Human Person; The Way That Leads There: Augustinian Reflections on the Christian Life; The Freedom of a Christian: Grace, Vocation, and the Meaning of Our Humanity; Bioethics: A Primer for Christians* (1996, 2005); *Body, Soul, and Bioethics,* and he is the editor (with William Werpehowski) of *The Oxford Handbook of Theological Ethics.*

INDEX

Imago Dei: Human Dignity in Ecumenical Perspective was designed in
Minion with Requiem display and typeset by Kachergis Book Design of
Pittsboro, North Carolina. It was printed on 60-pound Natures Recycled
and bound by McNaughton & Gunn of Saline, Michigan.